The Haskell Home Orphanage Tragedy
Battle Creek, Michigan

by

James N. Jackson

ISBN -13: 9798578986529

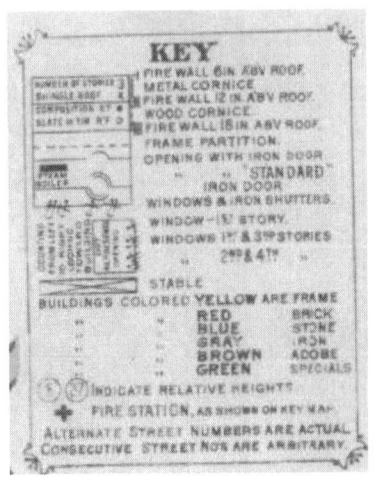

Cover Art:
Andrews University
Haskell Home, Battle Creek
Review & Herald Pub. Assn.
Neg. No. BB5422

Willard Library Historical Images
Haskell Home Fire, Feb. 5, 1909
LPC-035-014-002A

Back Cover Art:
Library of Congress
1899 Sanborn Fire Map from Battle Creek, Calhoun County, MI
http://hdl.loc.gov/loc.gmd/g4114bm.g039201899 [see key above]

Library of Congress
1919 Sanborn Fire Map from Battle Creek, Calhoun County, MI
http://hdl.loc.gov/loc.gmd/g4114bm.g039201919 [see key above]

https://www.loc.gov/resource/g4114bm.g039201919/?sp=71&r=-0.046,0.087,0.479,0.303,0

Printed in the United States of America
by kdp.amazon.com

Also available at Amazon.com
Barnesandnoble.com
and michlist.com

For Lee,

My best friend and wife for over fifty years

All the characters and events in this book are based on articles in local newspapers, periodicals and other contemporary sources listed in the bibliography.

Chapter 1.

The most famous fire in Battle Creek occurred in 1902. The Battle Creek Sanitarium, or the 'San' was completely destroyed, and through funds raised by the Seventh-day Adventist (S.D.A.) Church and Dr. John Harvey Kellogg, it was rebuilt. It is now the Hart-Dole-Inouye Federal Center.

This book is about another institution that was completely destroyed by fire only seven years later. There are many players that fit into the narrative of this story about an orphanage in Battle Creek, Michigan. The birth of the idea came from Dr. John H. Kellogg, in charge of the Battle Creek Sanitarium that Presidents, Royalty, Hollywood idols, and common folks frequented. His idea to restore health was by a natural diet, exercise, plenty of fresh air, and intellectual stimulation. He envisioned this healthy regiment in the orphanage as well.

Mrs. Caroline Haskell, a recent widow of some wealth, learned of his unfulfilled dream of an orphanage and donated the entire amount needed for the construction.

The S.D.A. led by James and Ellen White conducted annual pledge drives for the upkeep of the institution until a falling out with Dr. Kellogg caused the S.D.A. to withdraw those needed annual funds, thus jeopardizing the solvency of the Haskell Home.

And the fire that destroyed the "grandest institution in Battle Creek" in a matter of hours effectively ended the dream, consuming three young lives in the inferno.

If an orphanage in the 1890s brings to mind the conditions of a work house from Dickens or even the "Little Orphan Annie" comic strip during the Great Depression, that would not be far off. However, Dr. Kellogg, envisioned a sanctuary where every child was educated, exposed to world-class culture and assigned individual and group chores. With the children grouped into small families, their physical, mental, spiritual development, their diet and Dr. Kellogg's building ventilation system in place, it is safe to say that there was no other orphanage like the Haskell Home of Battle Creek. This sanctuary predated the Starr Commonwealth[1] and Boys Town, founded by Father Edward J. Flanagan.

Although called an orphanage, many children were not parentless. Some had both parents living but for various reasons, these parents could not care for all their children, at least for short periods of time. Some dropped off their children daily or for weeks at a time, while they worked or sought employment in other areas. The children were referred to as "inmates," a term retained in this publication.

The title for this publication came easily. The tragedy of the three children perishing in the 1909 fire certainly was horrific, but the concept to nurture the friendless by placing children into family units was unique at the time, and many of Dr. Kellogg's improvements for the care of these orphans were delayed from common use for many years as a result.

This publication moved forward due to the interest provided by Nick Buckley, Dave Eddy, Jack Gottlieb and Sherri Sherban. Their positive comments encouraged the conversion from an interesting story to a published book. Jody Owens, with her knowledge of Battle Creek history also offered corrections to the final draft.

This is the story of the rise and fall of the Haskell Home of Battle Creek run by John H. Kellogg. All the characters and events in this book are based on articles recorded in local newspapers, periodicals and other contemporary sources listed in the bibliography. Over a few short years, the Haskell Home found permanent homes for over 600 children and nurtured many more to adulthood.

For a Face-to-Face pre-publication interview with the author by host Dave Eddy on the Haskell Home Orphanage, see AccessVision episode #185 at accessvision.tv/file/15430.

---

[1] The Starr Commonwealth was founded in 1913 in Albion, Michigan, and Boys Town near Omaha, Nebraska, was established in 1917. The biography *Father Flanagan of Boys Town* by Oursler, mentioned "Floyd Starr, who established his Commonwealth for Boys," but there was no mention of the Haskell Home of Battle Creek.

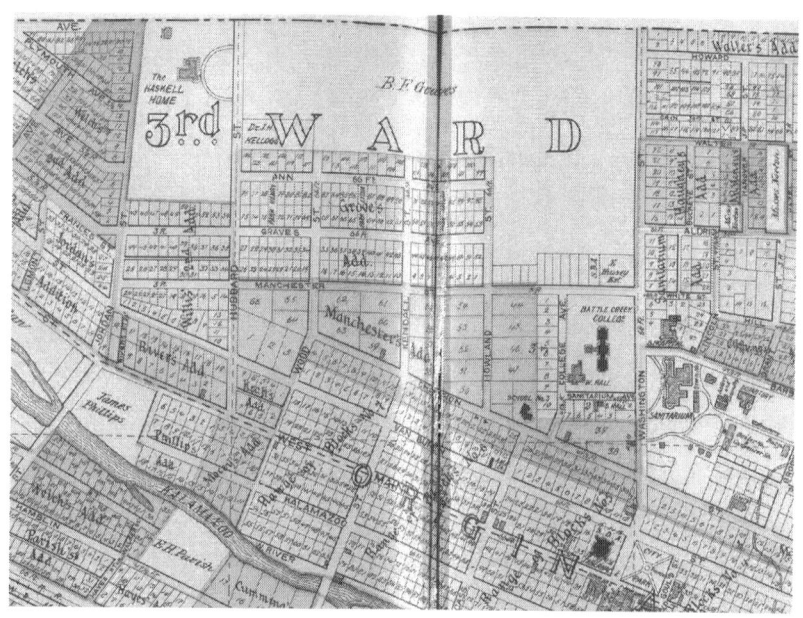

Part of the City of Battle Creek, 1894
Rare Book Room
Library of Michigan

The Haskell Home is located in the northwest quarter, with the
residence of Dr. John H. Kellogg across Hubbard St. The
S.D.A. Tabernacle and the Sanitarium are located in the
southeast quarter.

Chapter 2.

John Harvey Kellogg (1852-1943) & Ella (Eaton) Kellogg (1853-1920)
Historical Society of Battle Creek Archives

John H. Kellogg, was a medical doctor, nutritionist, inventor and health activist. He was the director of the Battle Creek Sanitarium[2] that was funded by members of the S.D.A. Church. It treated both the rich and famous and also the poor who could not afford other hospitals. He was a leader in progressive health reform and wrote extensively on science and health, combining scientific knowledge with Adventist beliefs, promoting health reform, temperance and sexual abstinence. This included a regiment of vegetarianism, nutrition, the use of enemas, exercise, sun-bathing, hydrotherapy, and abstention from smoking tobacco and drinking alcoholic beverages. The San was built in 1876 and during the previous two decades of the nineteenth century the institution became the largest of its kind in the world. Dr. Kellogg's beliefs about a healthful diet of whole grain foods, fruit and vegetables were incorporated in the meals prepared at the San. He invented what he called

---

[2] Dr. Kellogg coined the term "Sanitarium" from sanitorium and sanitarian, to suggest both hospital care and the importance of sanitation and personal health. He lead the institution until his death in 1943, never accepting a salary, just relying on his book royalties for income. The institution was named the San by locals.

granola, developed peanut butter,[3] and with his brother, Will Keith Kellogg, generally referred to as W. K. Kellogg, discovered a method of making wheat and corn flakes to be used in the Sanitarium meals. Beyond their physical well-being, outstanding entertainers and lecturers often entertained the guests. In 1884, Dr. Kellogg started a kindergarten class for children of the guests.

The Battle Creek Sanitarium, 1913.

Ella (Eaton) Kellogg was an American pioneer in dietetics. She was educated at Alfred University (B.A. 1872, A.M. 1875), the youngest person to receive a degree from that school. In 1875 she visited the Battle Creek Sanitarium, and became interested in the subjects of sanitation and hygiene, while caring for victims of a typhoid epidemic. She joined the editorial staff of *Good Health* Magazine and married Dr. John Harvey Kellogg in 1879 at the San.

She was prominently identified with the Woman's

---

[3] Several men are credited with inventing or discovering versions of peanut butter. Marcellus Gilmore Edson, a Canadian pharmacist patented peanut butter in 1884. Dr. Kellogg was issued a patent for a "Process of Producing Alimentary Products" in 1898, that used peanuts. *National Peanut Board.*

Christian Temperance Union (W.C.T.U.), in 1882 being appointed national superintendent of the Department of Hygiene. Her several books include *Science in the Kitchen* (1892) and *Studies in Character Building* (1905), the bible for child rearing for forty years.

She was inducted in the Michigan Women's Hall of Fame in 1999, for her achievements in philanthropist, nutrition and dietetics.

Daily drill for Sanitarium patients in the gymnasium
The Battle Creek Sanitarium Book, n.d.

Three thousand teachers enjoying a banquet in the same room
The Battle Creek Sanitarium Book, n.d.

Although they had no children of their own, their house always seemed full of little ones.[4] Ella asked the doctor to bring home a baby from New York the next time he went up and this was the beginning of his taking care of orphans. From time to time he came across children he wished to adopt and so would bring them home. They took forty homeless youngsters into their own personal quarters and financed the education of as many as thirty persons (at one time), while adopting twelve children. After a time he gathered so many about him that it was impossible to adequately care for them and so the idea of a home was conceived.

His interest was shared with Ellen G. White, the co-founder of the Seventh-day Adventist Church. In addressing the managers of the Battle Creek Sanitarium on Oct. 16, 1890 she counselled them:

> Dear Brethren: While in Petoskey [Michigan] I had some conversation with your physician in chief in regard to establishing a home for orphan children at Battle Creek. I said that this was just what was needed among us as a people, and that in enterprises of this kind we were far behind other denominations[5].

On March 22, 1891, Dr. Kellogg addressed the Adventist leadership assembled for the General Conference on the need of an orphanage in the city. In an emotion-packed address the doctor graphically portrayed some poignant cases which had come to his attention, and he indicated that a primitive survey which he had conducted showed that there were at least 225 Adventist orphans currently needing institutional care. Among other arguments in favor of an Adventist orphanage, Kellogg suggested that such an institution would be a splendid place to begin the preparation of workers for denominational service.

---

[4] According to the 1900 census, the Kellogg's were raising two wards from Pennsylvania, and eleven adopted children from California, Colorado, Illinois, Nebraska, Michigan and Mexico.

[5] Testimonies, vol. 8, p. 133.

"Resolved. That we believe a home for orphans and destitute persons to be called the "James White Memorial Home" should be established by this denomination, and further.

Resolved. That we recommend the General Conference to select a Committee of seven to take this matter under consideration immediately, with power to act, in conjunction with the General Conference Committee."

Dr. Kellogg was placed at the head of this committee charged to organize a home for orphan children and friendless aged persons. Although the original resolutions provided for just one home for both orphans and the elderly, as the Committee developed its plans it was decided to establish two homes – one for orphans and the other for the aged. The committee set about the work of collecting the necessary funds for this purpose. This included the organization of a general Medical Missionary and Benevolent Association for the purpose of assisting orphans, homeless aged persons, sick and needy persons of all classes and educating missionary physicians and nurses.

Finding no statute suitable for the incorporation of an association of such extensive aims and objects, a bill was presented to the Legislature providing for such an incorporation. Michigan was behind some other states in its provisions for the establishment of charitable enterprises, perhaps due to the fact that the state had no large cities at that time, as dense masses of impoverished people congregated in larger cities.

To be sure Michigan was foremost in many aspects of public beneficence. Its asylums for the blind, for the deaf and dumb, its State School, its Industrial School, its public school system, its great University, its State Reform School[6], were all

---

[6] To explain the national scene in the nineteenth century, Belle Starr was sent to Detroit for incarceration as it was the nearest facility for imprisonment of women "out west."

institutions of great merit, but what was missing was encouragement of private philanthropy on the part of its citizens.   These private funds would benefit   the State materially in reducing the number of charges sent to   poor houses, reform schools and other public institutions.

When the suggestion was first made for the building of an Orphans' Home, only a few thousand dollars was raised, and the promoters became somewhat discouraged. Even so, Dr. Kellogg purchased the site of the future Home with his own money.   Even without a building, the mere suggestion of provision for the helpless brought applications for admission and a group of homeless children began to arrive and were gathered into the Sanitarium Annex. Slowly but surely the family grew and soon additional helpers had to be secured and the eighteen rooms in the Annex were filled. Adding another location the facility was equipped with a nursery, kindergarten and primary school. The new site necessitated the pitching of a tent to increase the facilities of the temporary school.

Plans were made for a modest building which could later be expanded but still there was no money. The S.D.A. as a whole were as generous and perhaps surpassed other religions as they funded missionaries around the world with additional pledges in addition to their weekly contributions. However part of the resolution was the condition that a general subscription was forbidden and gifts of less than $100 could not be accepted, which greatly crippled any fund raising attempt. At this point, having a vision that was supported by the community, but lacking the needed funds was even more discouraging for Dr. Kellogg.

Christmas program at the San to promote the Haskell Home
Possibly taken in December, 1891.
Historical Society of Battle Creek Archives

Chapter 3.

Hon. Frederick Haskell (1810-1890)
and Mrs. Caroline E. Haskell (1822-1900)
Historical Society of Battle Creek Archives

Frederick Haskell was born December 4, 1810 at East Windsor, Connecticut, the son of Eli B. Haskell, a merchant of comfortable fortune. In 1831 he moved west and started the first general store in Princeton, Illinois. He sold his prosperous business and returned to New York to join his father at his flour mill in Ogdensburg. He was able to amass a considerable fortune that was lost by 1846 and having to start over, he again went west. He formed a partnership with Hiram Aldridge and Dr. Sherman, building freight cars in Michigan City, Indiana. During the war, the railroad business increased and the company grew. By 1879 the company had a payroll of 500 men and an output of 1,000 cars a year. The income from his company and investments in Chicago real estate, made him a millionaire before he retired in 1884. Frederick Haskell died on May 6, 1890.

Caroline was the daughter of Isaac Aldridge, born July 22, 1822 in New York. She married Frederick Haskell on November 11, 1852 in Chazy, New York.

For eighteen years she made her home in Chicago, "but Chicago was too fast and noisy for me so I came out here [Michigan City, Indiana] to a quiet home, where I expect to end my days."

After her husband died, Mrs. Haskell donated more than one million dollars to establish a hospital in Chicago, the Congregational Church of Chicago, The Congregational Church of Michigan City, Indiana, the Chicago Humane Society, University of Chicago[7], Oberlin College and to relatives.

In 1892, during a chance visit to Battle Creek to visit a friend at the San, she met Dr. Kellogg and offered to donate the entire funds required to build the orphanage in Battle Creek.

The Haskell Oriental Museum
ebay.com

---

[7]   The University of Chicago received $20,000 for lectures in comparative religion and $100,000 for the Haskell Oriental Museum for Middle East Studies in her husband's name. The museum was also known as Haskell Hall.

Research Archives – Library
The Oriental Institute of the University of Chicago
oi.uchicago.edu/research/research-archives-library

Chapter 4.

In April of 1892, Mrs. Caroline E. Haskell was visiting the Battle Creek Sanitarium with some friends. Impressed with the operation of this vast complex she called on Dr. Kellogg to find out more about his work. She told him that she was "pleased by what she had seen and heard," and would like to assist the work by leaving a few thousand dollars. Surprised, and doubting whether he had heard correctly, Dr. Kellogg was at a loss as to what to think, but began to explain about the endowed beds at the Sanitarium.

Mrs. Haskell informed him she was interested in something larger than this. Noting the astonished look on the doctor's face, she explained:

> Perhaps you doubt my ability to do what I propose. As I am a perfect stranger to you, I may perhaps properly explain that my husband died two years ago and left me with considerable property – much more than I could ever use myself, and I have found it a pleasure to give to worthy enterprises such as I have thought my husband would have been willing to encourage if he were living."[8]

Dr. Kellogg then remarked that another enterprise which was in still greater need of assistance than the Hospital work was a home for orphans, for which he had been for some months trying to raise money, hoping to get an amount sufficient to erect a building to suitably care for the children of both sexes and all ages who were pleading for entrance.

"That is just such an enterprise as I should like to assist, and I should like to talk with you further in reference to your plans."

A few days later Mrs. Haskell examined the plans which had already been prepared and recognized that they were insufficient for the purpose, and might be greatly improved. After some thought, she made a proposition which startled the

---

[8] *Medical Missionary Year Book*, 1896.

doctor, coming so lately as a stranger to the project. She planned to support the entire building herself, at a cost of $30,000, provided it might stand as a memorial to her deceased husband. She explained that Mr. Haskell had reared more than one orphan lad to manhood, and contributed many thousands of dollars to institutions for boys.[9]

New designs were prepared based on her suggestions and submitted for her approval, and by midsummer the funds were in the hands of the committee. Her only conditions were that the building should bear her husband's name, that the work should be conducted in a broad and liberal spirit so that its benefits should not be confined within sectarian lines.

Although Mrs. Haskell was an Episcopalian, she had an interest in a variety of religions around the world and had no qualms regarding the S.D.A. committee in charge of the project. She agreed with the arrangement that the Orphans' Home be under the same management as had been planned from the conception of the work. She gave the money outright, without asking any voice in its management, or other restrictions, except the naming of the institution and that it be nonsectarian.

William Conqueror Sisley (1850-1932) was the architect and builder. He was also the architect of the original Battle Creek Sanitarium, Battle Creek College, and other buildings in South Africa, Australia and England.[10]

---

[9] Mrs. E. H. Henry, "A Sketch of Mr. Haskell," MM, February, 1894.

[10] Contemporary sources listed either Mr. Sisley or A. D. Ordway as architect and builder of the Haskell Home. Mr. Ordway built scores of homes, and was the architect of the central fire station, the Trump, Phoenix, Tacoma and Morgan blocks and the Roosevelt School. He is also mentioned as the architect of the old Haskell Home in the August 5, 1956 edition of the Battle Creek *Enquirer and News*. The biography of William C. Sisley in the *The Missionary Worker*, October 21, 1932 listed him as the architect of the Haskell Home in Battle Creek. Sources list both as

The Hall Brothers of Battle Creek built the foundation under contract. All of the carpenter work, painting and plumbing was done by the day under the supervision of Wm C. Sisley, who bought all material.

E. P. Dexter came from College View, Nebraska to take charge of the crew of men erecting the Haskell Orphan's Home, September 17, 1892. Construction progressed rapidly, with the stone work of the first story nearly completed by September 28. Excavations were also made at that time for the nearby boiler and engine room. By December 20, the roof enclosed the building, making the building ready for windows. During the winter the inside work was carried forward as far as possible and walls were plastered in early spring. The building was completed January 20, 1894.

The grounds comprised seventeen acres[11] which were set out with trees, and in time would become a beautiful park. Just north was a fifty acre field which belonged to the association.

The site was a commanding one. Situated on an elevation which overlooked the river valley, it could be seen by all the passengers going West or East on the three railroads. From the railroad car window it presented an imposing appearance.

Visitors at the 1893 World's Fair[12] in Chicago could visit the exhibit of the Sanitarium hospital model placed side-by-side with the model of the Haskell Home for orphans.

---

architect or builder, and it is difficult which person was in charge, assuming that they were both involved.

[11] By 1901 the farm consisted of 67 acres, with 1,200 peach, 1,000 plum, 300 pear and several hundred apple trees, five acres of strawberries (which produced 10,000 quarts), seven acres of raspberries, one acre of currants and gooseberries and a vineyard of grapes. $345 worth of produce was sold in this season. By 1905 the orchard consisted of over 2,000 peach trees.

[12] Also known as the World's Columbian Exposition and Chicago Columbian Exposition. Afterwards, this model made from the builder's plans was on display on the fifth floor parlor of the Sanitarium.

The building faced south and east 117 feet on each side, and was three stories and an attic high above the basement. The foundation was wood, brick veneered. The caps and sills of the windows and other trimmings were of buff lime stone. The roof was half pitch Gothic. On each side were two dormer windows with two on the back side. Ventilators were located on the west and north ends.

There was an imposing veranda fourteen feet wide and twelve feet high, the whole length of the west and south side, a total of 300 feet, which made a pleasant promenade.

A daily scene in the kitchen
Haskell Home Appeal Vol. I, No. 1 – October 1897

There were four entrances to the basement and four to the first floor. The main entrance was at the south corner of the north wing, on the first floor facing Hubbard Street.

The basement was 11 feet high, containing a dining room 40 by 65 feet; a kitchen 22 by 28; a business office 16.4 by 19.10; a commissary department consisting of three rooms as follows: fruit room 13 by 20, creamery 9 by 10, store room 15.5 by 32.8. Boys' closet 14.6 by 21.6; lavatory 11.9 by

21.10; bath room 26.5 by 22; girls bath room and lavatory 17 by 33.6; gardener's room 15 by 16. There were four private rooms, one each for the gardener and cooks. There was also a reception hall and cloak room[13] for the boys; a storage room for linens and a room to keep the children's outer wraps[13]. The kitchen had a row of sinks in graduated heights and spaces between the sinks for dishes.

In the Sloyd Room
Haskell Home Appeal Vol. VIII, No. 3 – April 1905

On the first floor was a hall 18 by 18.11; reception parlors 24.5 by 25.7; assembly room, 39 by 41; gymnasium 22 by 28; Sloyd room[14] 18 by 24.2. There were three school

---

[13] The defininition for male and female attire at the time – **Cloak**: a loose outer garment, such as a coat, hat, etc. **Wrap**: a loose outer garment of a woman. Chamber's *Twentieth Century Dictionary*, 1904.

[14] The tern Sloyd, is generally understood to mean a system of handwork in wood. It differs from carpentry in several essential features. There is no division of labor in Sloyd. Carpentry is a trade, and the principles which underlie it are entirely utilitarian, whereas Sloyd is solely a means of Formative Education. Its purpose is not to turn out carpenters, but to develop the mental, moral, and physical powers

rooms; one 24.5 by 27; one 20 by 34.5; one 16 by 26; girls closet 15.3 by 28; lavatory 11.9 by 28; matron's private room 12.5 by 17.

On the second floor was a library corner 24.5 by 25.7; sewing room for girls, 17 by 20; four suites of rooms, a sitting room, 17.2 by 18; dormitory 29.10 by 18; chamber 10.2 by 16; wardrobe 7.4 by 16. Each one of these suites of rooms accommodated the matron and twelve orphans. There were twelve single iron bedsteads in the dormitory.

There was also a nursery 16 by 25 and a dormitory 16 by 21.3; attendant's room 11 by 18, and babies' bath room 9 by 6.1. On this floor was a quarantine room for all new comers 16.8 by 28, with closets and wash basins. All children brought to the Home were cared for in quarantine a certain length of time until they were free from disease.

The third floor was similar to the second floor with the addition of the following: Four private rooms for teachers, 14 by 16; boys' sewing room, 17 by 20.4. A contagious disease room 16.3 by 28, with bath room, closet and wash-room all separated from the other part of the building by four doors.

In the attic were two private rooms 16 by 16; two rainy day play rooms (one for the girls and one for the boys) 24 by 72 and two store rooms 12 by 40.

In the open tower was the observatory, where a magnificent view could be obtained of Battle Creek and surrounding country, especially of the Kalamazoo river valley.

The inside work of the Home was finished in long leafed southern or yellow pine, which made a very beautiful finish.

The Home could accommodate 150 orphans. There were already thirty orphans in the city looking forward to becoming occupants of the new home after completion. They occupied the old Sanitarium Annex on Barbour Street, but were removed to the Haughey residence on Aldrich Street, which had been fitted up for their occupancy.

---

of children; and it is the most effective instrument yet devised for securing this development. Otoo A. Salomon, *The Theory of Educational Sloyd*, 1906.

Boys' Dormitory and Sitting-Room
Haskell Home Appeal Vol. I, No. 1 – October 1897

The Nursery Family
Haskell Home Appeal Vol. I, No. 3 – April 1898

The Kindergarten
Haskell Home Appeal Vol. 7, No. 3 – October 1903

The building was ventilated by Dr. Kellogg's system. It was heated by steam and lighted by electricity by a separate boiler room located 100 feet northwest of the building and was 60 by 60. This building contained the boilers for heating, the electric light plant and the laundry.

Class in Kitchengarden, Haskell Home
Historical Society of Battle Creek Archives

First Lesson in Cookery, Haskell Home
Historical Society of Battle Creek Archives

Although it snowed the day before, the sun shone on the public exercises of the dedication of the Haskell Home for Orphans held on Thursday, January 25, 1894. There was a very large attendance and the order of exercises were as follows: Invocation; anthem by sanitarium chorus; history of the enterprise by Dr. J. H. Kellogg; sketch of the life of Frederick Haskell by Mrs. E. H. Shigndy; dedicatory address by Bishop George D. Gillespie, superintendent state board of charities; anthem; scriptural reading, with responses by the children, and dedicatory prayer by Elder L. McCoy. Dr. Kellogg explained that one of the characteristics of this Home would be to create a home atmosphere for the children by dividing the entire family into small groups, each group having its own Mother. The house was constructed with suites of apartments, instead of a large dormitory. "Each suite is large enough for a family of twelve or thirteen children, and no more than that number are intended to be placed in a single family. Each Mother will remain with her family ... until they grow up and are prepared to go out and make their own way in the world." Children would attend school together in their appropriate grades, and they would all eat in the dining room together, sitting at their own family table. Otherwise they spent the remaining time within their own family unit.

The orphanage would "rear the children ... to give them such an education as to make them whole men and whole women. The girls, as well as the boys will be taught trades."

Bishop Gillespie, chairman of the state board of charities, said:

There is one thing, friends, I desire especially to say to you, and that is these little ones will never want for bread. If ever your treasury gets empty, all you have to do is to show these little ones to the public and kind-hearted men and women will be moved to open their pocketbooks and supply you with funds for their necessities.

This was followed by the anthem; inspection of the building; and exercises by the children in the assembly room. After the exercises the visitors were taken on a tour through the building. Visitors continued to show up to tour the institution, becoming a hindrance to the children and workers. In May, 1894, Dr. Kellogg published a plea in the local newspaper asking persons intending to visit the Haskell Home to please note regular visiting hours, and schedule a tour. By 1895, tours were scheduled throughout the year.

Photo from Duff Stoltz collection
Courtesy of Joyce Stoltz

In 1894, both the Sanitarium and the Haskell Home placed an order with Evan D. Hubbard, agent for the Gamewell Fire Alarm Company of New York to equip these institutions with auxiliary fire alarm boxes. These boxes were about one fourth the size of ordinary street boxes and arranged that by pulling down a ring in any one of the boxes would send an alarm to the fire department.

The General Conference set aside special Sabbaths twice a year for Maintenance Fund collections. In 1897 *The Haskell Home Appeal* was begun to assist in raising funds for upkeep.

At the close of the decade of the 1890s, 318 children had been cared for in the Haskell Home, 186 boys and 132 girls – the youngest deposited at the Home when a babe of only a few hours. Of these children 153 were returned to relatives able to assume care of them. 13 had been adopted and 112 were still living at the Home.[15]

The superintendent and his wife only received their board, no salary. Those who cared for the children gave their first year's service free; the second year they received $12 a month, and thereafter $15 per month. The teachers received $12 each month.

---

[15] These figures do not include children placed in homes through the relief department.

Chapter 5.

From the beginning it was the purpose of the managers of this Home to make it much more a genuine home for children than had ever before been attempted in similar institutions. The entire family of little ones would be divided into families of twelve, each one under the charge of a missionary Mother or caretaker.[16] Each person connected with the Home, from the cook to the caretakers and the teachers, before undertaking their duties would complete a course of training in the Sanitarium. The purpose would be to make the Home not simply a temporary stopping place for children, but a place in which boys and girls would be exposed to culture, trained to a self-supporting age, receive a good education, instructed through manual training in one or more trades, and develop any skills that individual talents might suggest.

Special attention for the physical health of the little ones, an abundance of the best food[17] prepared in the most wholesome manner, plenty of exercise in the open air, daily gymnastics and other hygienic means contributed to the development of a high state of physical health.

Each "Mother" completed the Mothers' Training Class. The instruction in medical lines was given by physicians and other teachers from the Sanitarium. This included a course in Physiology and Hygiene, and also in Practical Nursing. These were followed by courses in Hydrotherapy, practical and theoretical, Children's Diseases, Accidents and Emergencies, etc. A series of lessons on Domestic Science by Mrs. Ella Kellogg, and classes in sewing and cooking were included.

Physical Culture and a class in Kindergarten, Principles of Christian Education and Character Building, the latter conducted by Mrs. Kellogg were open to all who cared to attend and were always popular.

---

[16] Older boys had a Father, rather than a Mother.

[17] Meat was a staple from the beginning, but the meals became completely vegetarian by the turn of the century, in keeping with the recommended S.D.A. diet.

Dr. Kellogg recognized the need for a three-fold (physical, mental and spiritual) development so that the children would develop equally in each. The Home attempted to give attention to all these needs. In the first issue of *The Haskell Home Appeal*, a schedule of events was printed as of October 1897:

A company of one hundred and eleven children, from two weeks to sixteen years of age, are formed into eight families, with a Father for the larger boys, and Mothers for the girls and smaller children. Each family is furnished a suite of rooms, consisting of sitting-room, dormitory, care-taker's room, and clothes-room.

The morning bell rings at 5 A.M., and all rise. One hour and thirty minutes are spent with the toilette, sweeping halls, and putting the house in order. A few strokes of the bell brings all the families to their rooms from 6:30 to 6:45 A.M. for silent meditations or reading of Scripture. From 6:45 to 7:45 A.M. all the families meet in the chapel for instruction from the word of God, and for prayer.

The children march two by two to the dining-room, where the family idea is emphasized. Each family has its own table and chairs, which are arranged according to the size of the children.

A good diet of grains prepared in a variety of ways, with nuts and fruit, constitutes the usual bill of fare. After breakfast, the work of the day begins.

The members of each family, under the direction of the care-taker, work both indoors and out in their gardens for a few hours, after which comes the play hour.

Listening to the Bible story
Haskell Home Appeal, Vol. 7, No. 3, Oct. 1903

Nursery, Haskell Home
Historical Society of Battle Creek Archives

Dinner[18] is served at 2 P.M., followed by work and play, until the bell calls the children to their rooms for worship. They next prepare for bed and a good night's rest.

Sabbath[19], at 11 A.M., the children are taken to the Sanitarium chapel to listen to the sermon, thus affording them a pleasant change in the weekly routine.

The children were taught to help in many ways by performing household duties, boys as well as girls. Tots of four and five made their own beds and from this advanced to sweeping, dusting, washing dishes and helping with the laundry. The children had daily lessons, not merely from their primers, arithmetics, and physiologies, but also at the tables set with plain, healthful food, in the spacious kitchen where they were taught to prepare the food and wash the dishes, and on the adjoining farm where they learned to till the soil.

They entered kindergarten at three years of age. Mrs. A. C. Kingman was the director of the Haskell Home kindergarten and participated in a public meeting on March 27, 1896, for the express purpose of establishing a free kindergarten within the public schools of Battle Creek.

The fifth grade arithmetic class, while studying square measure, took measurements of the gymnasium and determined the cost of painting its walls.

About twenty-two of the boys in the upper grades were in the wood sloyd classes, and learned the use of tools and many other practical lessons.

The sewing class was graded, and both boys and girls began with the first model. These lessons taught the different stitches used in sewing, beginning with basting. They included darning, patching, and sewing on buttons. The girls were expected to complete twenty-six models, by which time they

---

[18] The two meals were breakfast and dinner. Dinner was the chief meal of the day.

[19] This was Saturday in keeping with the S.D.A.'s observance of the seventh day of the week.

became familiar with the implements and processes of plain sewing. The boys were not taught the more advanced models, as the object was to teach them to care for and keep in repair their own garments so that they would not be helpless if they were ever left without feminine resources. The girls were taught how to use tools.

A class in chair caning & mattress making
Haskell Home Appeal, Vol. 7, No. 3, Oct. 1903

Boys were taught chair caning and mattress making.

It was the aim of the management to teach the children the value of work itself. They were taught punctuality, method and neatness. Their duty to society and to the church was also emphasized. Much attention was paid to the selection of food since this exerted such an influence over physical health and habit.

Haskell Home Children at Work on the Farm
Haskell Home Appeal Vol. I, No. 1 – October 1897

Our Beet Field
The Haskell Home Appeal, Vol. 4, No. 1, Oct. 1900

Group of Haskell Home Children
Historical Society of Battle Creek Archives

Photo from Duff Stoltz collection
Courtesy of Joyce Stoltz

During 1900, the Haskell Home engaged in the cultivation of sugar beets. A gentleman well educated in beet culture ventures asserted that the crop would yield 15 tons to the acre. Under a contract with the sugar factory at Kalamazoo, the children harvested twenty acres of beets. The field was divided into two large pieces, one containing about twelve acres, and the other eight. Each field was hoed four times. It gave the children good healthy exercise and they seemed to enjoy the work. One of the lads hoed nine rows across the ten acre plat in one day, but none of them were set to any forced quota. It was hoped that the field would pay out well to the Home when the crop was harvested. The accompanying picture was taken by request of a representative of the sugar factory.

There were eighty-five children[20] residing in the Haskell Home, caring for cows, and chickens, and busy making preparations for planting peas, potatoes, sweet corn, and other garden vegetables, and caring for strawberry vines, raspberry plants and other small fruits.

Boys left the institution at an earlier age than the girls. Girls were usually about eighteen when they made their way in the world. Sometimes they assumed support of a dependent relative.

During the difficult year of 1908, when the S.D.A. withheld financial support, there was a discussion regarding sending inmates into the public schools for their education. It was the opinion of the trustees that these children would be considered foreign in the sense of the law and would have to pay tuition, so the Haskell home maintained its own education system.

All these endeavors, both in the Home and outside in the fields contributed to the goal of providing trades and instill valuable work ethics for the children, as well as providing some small profit to supplement the charitable donations that benefited both the Home and the children.

---

[20] *The Bible Echo*, Vol. 2, No. 28, page 221, July 30, 1896

A family playground
The *Haskell Home Appeal*, Vol. 7, No. 1, Oct. 1903

Chapter 6.

Top row: Lois Randall, Nina Fleetwood, Alline Swartout
Next to top row: Unknown, Anna Frey, Martha Johnson, unknown
In Center: Miss Sarah Bean (Caretaker)
Next to bottom: Alta Gestner, Sophie Termeir?, Josie Hyatt, Effie
Turner
Bottom row: Alice Frey[21], Jessie Turner
Andrews University Archives (c. 1905)

The children brought to the Home were from a variety of nationalities, races and personalities. They came from what was then said to be the "lowest and most forlorn conditions of life."

Word got out from local papers, the *Haskell Home Appeal* and in Adventist church bulletins. There are no records of where the children came from directly but according to the 1900 census, their place of births included twenty-five of the then forty-five states, namely Alabama, Connecticut, Colorado, Florida, Illinois, Iowa, Indiana, Kansas, Louisiana, Massachusetts, Michigan, Minnesota, Missouri, Nebraska, New Jersey, New York, Ohio, Pennsylvania, Tennessee, Texas,

---

[21] Alice Frey, with short black hair, cut when she had typhoid fever.

Virginia, Vermont, Washington, West Virginia, Wisconsin and also India, Mexico, Nova Scotia and Puerto Rico.

Not all children were orphans, but all came from families who were desperate and no longer able to care for their children, at least temporarily.

There were many stories of inmates and their interaction with the neighboring community in the local papers. A few examples follow that should provide a glimpse of life in a small town at the turn of the century.

An article in the *Kalamazoo Gazette* reported the capture of an insane man, James McFarren, in May of 1897. He was arrested in Battle Creek about two years before for the larceny of a load of hay from a farmer in Climax, which he then sold in Battle Creek. He escaped from an asylum in Ohio. His wife was a domestic in Battle Creek and their children, Calita, age 11, and Henry, age 5 were living at the Haskell Home.[22]

In April of 1899, Mrs. A. T. Rosser found a small boy about eight years old wandering about the streets near the west end park, who was unable to tell where he belonged. He was taken to the police department where he said his name was William Sherman Gibson and claimed that he lived with his Mother in a house on Maple Street. Officer McCoy, after questioning the boy, found that he had been living at the Haskell Home part of the time, and the remainder with his Mother on the north side of the city. She worked out by the day and left the youngster alone. He was taken to the Haskell Home and cared for at that place. The caretakers stated that the boy had been missing from the premises since the previous morning.

Alvah Rogers of Lansing and Mrs. German of this city got into a verbal argument in front of the police department, Sunday afternoon, June 18, 1899. Mrs. German claimed to have adopted Mr. Rogers nine-year-old nephew but was no relation to him. Mr. Rogers didn't believe her and thinking

---

[22] These children were still at the Haskell Home in the 1900 census.

him ill treated, as he was bare foot and dirty, attempted to take him home with him. They got into a tugging war with the child in the middle. The police interfered and discovered that the management of the Haskell Home had been lawfully instructed to take charge of the youth, and the two parties left empty-handed.

Mrs. Ada Park and children, who had spent eight months at the Haskell Home, returned to their home in Chicago, October 29, 1900.[23]

Two little children named Bronson[24] were taken to Punta Gorda, Florida by a Mr. Cook, who brought them up and gave them a home.

In December of 1902, a short time after Mrs. Mabel Mull placed her 20 month-old son in the Haskell Home, the Home gave the child to Edward Rickner of this city. The Mother regained her child on a writ of habeas corpus.

At the beginning of May, 1903, Albert Peters, about eight years old, arrived in Battle Creek via the M.C.R.R., having travelled alone from Hartford, Connecticut. Police officer Godsmark happened to be at the depot when the 3:30 train from the East came into the station, and the little fellow was turned over to him by the porter. He presented a letter to the officer which stated that he was on his way to the Haskell Home.

In March, 1906, G. Hagele and J. Niles transported seven children from the Haskell Home to Bowdle, South Dakota,

---

[23] The 1900 census shows Ada A. Park, 32; with Roy F., 14; Edith W., 7; Orl R., 2, and Hallie Park, age 4 months.

[24] Eugene and Lenoria Bronson, of Punta Gorda, Florida had one son, Leslie Herman, born December 9, 1892, and twins Katie Bessie and Janie E., born June 13, 1896, all in Punta Gorda, Florida. Lenoria died September 26, 1900, in Punta Gordo, Florida, at the age of 26. Katie died as a child, August 26, 1901 in Battle Creek, Michigan, and was buried at Indian Springs cemetery, Punta Gorda, Florida. Mr. Cook was apparently returning Leslie, age 9 and Janie, age 5 to their father.

where they found homes on farms near that place: Clara Moore, Laura Wood, Willie Baird, Frank Gray, George Cady, Erwin Cady and LaVerne Millen. Although they were not adopted they were cared for until they were old enough to look after themselves. The children were all younger then twelve years of age.

In December of 1908, Pearl and Leon Counterman[25] made a complaint to the police department that their stepfather, David Tio, a junk dealer, had mistreated them and not allowed them to go to school. They were removed to the Haskell Home, where they were taken under the orders of County Agent Hillis. They were to remain there, together with a sister, until proper homes could be found for them.

A week later, Mrs. Alferetta Tio, of Park Street, engaged J. L. Powers to fight to retain the possession of her three children, named Counterman. If the jury decided they were neglected children, Probate Judge Hamm would secure desirable homes in which the children would be placed.

The trial revealed that the two little boys appeared at the police station one stormy evening, ragged, hungry and dirty and told a pitiful story of abuse and neglect.

While on their way to pick up coal one cold night, Leon and Pearl, aged thirteen and fifteen years respectively left their cart outside the station door while they mustered up courage to tell of the whippings they had received from the hands of their step-father, David Tio, a junk collector, and how they were kept out of school and compelled to assist in picking up junk in the alleys in the downtown districts.

Upon investigation, the police officers found conditions warranted the removal of the children from their squalid surroundings and accordingly the two boys with their fifteen year old sister were placed under the care of County Agent Hillis, pending an examination.

The three children appeared in court where they

---

[25] Pearl and Clarissa would have been have been 15 years old, Leon 13 at the end of 1907.

confronted their Mother and step-father together and apart sat their own father. Their Mother carried a young baby with her. The little waifs didn't seem to recognize their Mother and foster Father and their behavior bore out their repeated declarations that they didn't want to be sent back home.

Chief Farrington and Patrolmen Colby, Edmonds and Perry attended the hearing and testified in the case. These officers had often seen the little children hanging around the alleys, picking up rotten fruit and vegetables, and eating the same, so hungry were they. The Mother and stepfather were opposed to having the children taken away, while their own father was on hand to favor such a course.

Mrs. Laura Sprague brought two of her children to the Haskell Home in October, 1908 stating that she was unable to care for them, and arranged to make a certain payment for their board. Another child was left with Mrs. A. Farmington of Harrison Street by the Mother, who was also taken to the Haskell Home during the month of November. The woman stating that Mrs. Sprague had not complied with the agreement made when she took the youngster in.

The boys Jose, Kirk and Carl, were ten, seven and five years old respectively. Their father was dead. When the Mother left the little ones at the institution she was poorly clad and to all appearances her story of struggle and privation were true. Subsequent statements which came to the attention of Superintendent Rodney S. Owen created the suspicion in the minds of the officers that conditions were different now.

During the three months that the children were at the Haskell Home, the Mother had been to see them but once since she brought them there according to Superintendent Owen, and contributed little to their support, although she was in the city most of the time. Mrs. Sprague was the woman who had George Payne, a butcher for whom she kept house, arrested in August stating that he had threatened to kill her. Payne was then living in Flint according to County Agent Hillis who stated that a short time before he appeared at Haskell Home and demanded that the children be delivered into his charge.

The unnatural behavior of Mrs. Laura Sprague of placing her three little sons in the Haskell Home and then failing to make provisions for their care or even to visit them, prompted Superintendent R. S. Owen of that institution to petition the probate court to have the children adjudged delinquent, and placed out in homes. County Agent Hillis investigated the case.

December, 1908, was a busy month for County Agent Hillis, as he was in Clarendon, to remove three dependent children of Mrs. A. Needham to the county home. He stated that Mrs. Needham left her husband and unable to provide the little ones with suitable winter clothes to go to school. The truant officer reported the case to Supervisor Sherman, who instead of providing them with clothes, placed them in the county home. Mr. Hillis had the children transferred to the Haskell Home, pending a hearing of the case.

In January of 1909, a little lad less than four years old[26] arrived at the Battle Creek station with a note pinned to his coat, "Please help me to Haskell Home, Battle Creek, Michigan. My name is Stephen Chovin. I am from Worth, Michigan[27]." The little fellow was put off the train at this station where a Sanitarium porter found him, sobbing and trembling with fright. Tightly clasped under his arm was a satchel, in which his grandma put something to eat. The porter brought him to the Sanitarium where he was transferred to the Haskell Home.

In February, 1911, the Haskell Home was filled to capacity with about fifty boys and girls, including two sets of twins. One pair had been at the home for some time and named Earl and Pearl, five years old.[28] The other set, both

---

[26] Stephen was born on March 25, 1905, making him two months shy of four years of age.

[27] Worth, Michigan is over 200 miles east, located in the thumb area of the mitten state.

[28] Earl and Pearl DeWitt were born in 1905 according to the 1910 census.

girls, were only three months of age and had been at the Home since they were three weeks old. After much discussion, the Home decided to name them Eve and Iva.[29]

Mrs. Almira S. Steele, a great friend of Dr. and Mrs. J. H. Kellogg, was a guest at the Sanitarium in 1912. She was the founder and manager of the Steele Home for Orphans, a home for destitute colored children in Chattanooga, TN. She sought treatment at the Sanitarium for a broken wrist, her first vacation in twenty-eight years. She brought with her several children from the home and placed them in the Haskell Home. Over the years she sent 128 of her finished students to the Haskell Home, the Sanitarium, the College and other places, including one who became a private nurse for Booker T. Washington.

In December, 1912, Daniel and Cora Warner divorced and Mrs. Warner was granted custody of their child, Russell. Later, Mr. Warner alleged that his former wife notified him that he could have the boy. The thirteen-year-old boy was returned to his Mother's care who placed him in the Haskell Home.

Maud and Albert Needham were married in 1899, but in December, 1912 she sought a divorce, based on her husband's frequent intoxication and his abuse. He refused to provide for her and their two girls, and since she was hardly able to provide for herself, she placed her children in the Haskell Home. Both girls were adopted by families, one in Union City while the whereabouts of the other girl was unknown.

In 1931, local police were searching for a former inmate of the Haskell Home for an inheritance matter, involving a real estate agent in Pittsburg, Kansas. A ten dollar reward was offered for finding Eugene Wesley Blandin, thought to be an orphan at the Home from 1893 to 1901, born about 1887.

---

[29] Eve and Iva Campbell. Iva died June 15, 1911, six months old, from measles. Eva died April 5, 1912, aged 1 year and 4 months, from pleural pneumonia.

While in Battle Creek, Blandin went by the first name of Wesley, to distinguish him from another boy named Eugene.

These examples illustrate that there was not just one path to the Haskell Home in Battle Creek. Some came on their own, some were dropped off, some stayed for days, many lived there for years. All were provided with food, shelter, an opportunity to learn a trade, and the opportunity to become contributing members of society.

Chapter 7.

A Winter Scene
The Haskell Home Appeal, Vol. 3, No. 3, April 1900

There were constant activities, both in and around the Haskell Home, that included picnics at the lake, runaway horses in the neighborhood, and world-class entertainment at the San. The orphans walked to the San two-by-two for these events and joined the adults in attendance. Many of these events were also fundraisers for the Home.

On Monday, September 5, 1898, the Sanitarium celebrated the thirty-second anniversary of its founding. About nine thousand invitations were issued to friends and former guests of the institution. Carriages were provided so that guests could visit the Haskell Home, James White Memorial Home, and Dr. Kellogg's residence. After the dinner the guests came and went at will.

At the Haskell Home the children had on neat garments and enjoyed themselves as they played outside. Each family had its own playground and its own missionary garden.

On June 15, 1899 a picnic was held at Goguac Lake for the 200 Haskell Home children and they were given free rides on Captain Orton's steamer.

Perhaps not as much fun, but still important, in October, 1899, Dr. Harry T. Harvey did all the dental work for the hundred Haskell Home children free of charge, undertaking this of his own accord.

About twenty boys enjoyed a picnic at St. Mary's Lake on August 5, 1900. The children enjoyed bathing. In the afternoon Roy Rounds, a nine-year-old boy drowned, his story is detailed in chapter 9.

In December, 1900, about one hundred orphans gave a program of entertainment in the assembly room with the board of lady managers as their audience.

Goguac Lake Steamer "City of Battle Creek"
Willard Library Digital Collections, r03_0206.

In July, 1901, the Union Steam Pump Company Nine and the Banners played a game of baseball on the Haskell Home grounds. It was a hotly-fought game, enjoyed by all. This was followed in two days by fourteen of the boys travelling on the Lake Avenue cars to the Sanitarium villa for a day of fun at the lake. The boys had a dinner at the villa and spent the afternoon having a good time on their outing.

Prof. F. E. Belden gave the little folks at the Haskell Home some lessons in singing and taught them an original nature song written especially for them. Prof. Belden wrote several songs for the children and published them.

Owing to a shortage of coal, the fires at the Haskell Home were allowed to go out at night, so a request was printed in the December 10, 1902 *Battle Creek Daily Moon* to supply the Haskell Home with one hundred blankets for the orphan children, half-woolen blankets preferred. It went on to state that contributions of blankets or money may be left at Mr. Kelleher's dry goods store. The notice also reminded the citizens of Battle Creek that the institution was a very worthy one and that the institution had no endowment.

This may not have generated all the blankets required, because on January 8, 1903, members of the Woman's League met to tie comforts for the Haskell Home and served a 10¢ supper.

On May Day, 1903, the Haskell Home children toured the woods on a five mile hike for the first of the spring flowers. The blossoms were prettily arranged in small baskets made by the children and sent to the patients at Nichols Memorial Hospital.

On May 28, 1903, a large group of children from the Haskell Home enjoyed a picnic at Goguac Lake.

Children and young people celebrated the New Year of 1904 by presenting entertainment at the Haskell Home, which was enjoyed by the teachers and caretakers. Songs and recitations were included on the program.

In January of 1904, August Kapp, of Kapp Clothing Company hoped to draw customers into his store by passing out keys to a bank of money in his store – the shopper with the lucky key that opened the vault would win the money inside. If no one came forward with the winning key, half the money was going to go to the Nichols Memorial Hospital and the other half to the Haskell Home. There were pleas (advertisements) for several weeks, but no resolution was printed.

A spirited team of horses belonging to the Haskell Home became frightened at loose paper blowing about and started at a terrific speed down Manchester Street to Washington Avenue, turning off on West Van Buren Street, up Calhoun, and didn't stop until reaching Poplar Street, when a pedestrian caught the runaways. Fortunately no one was injured, although many narrow escapes were reported, especially when the animals crossed North Avenue, barely missing two young ladies who were on their way downtown.

In June, 1904, a team belonging to Mr. K. S. Cummings of the Haskell Home ran away from Peterson's plumbing shop on Washington Avenue. One of the animals was injured and the tongue of the wagon broken before they were stopped. Mr. Cummings was arrested the next day on the charge of leaving his team unhitched on the streets. He was arraigned before Recorder Hamm and pleaded not guilty.

On a Saturday morning in June, the orphans of the Haskell Home gave a very delightful and interesting program which consisted of recitations and music at the Battle Creek gymnasium.

That fall, Sister Ellen White stopped in Battle Creek on her way to the camp meeting in Nebraska. While waiting for the children to gather, her carriage was driven around through the orchard and farm. She enjoyed the drive, and spoke with appreciation of the farm and orchard, and the care that had been bestowed upon them. At the Haskell Home she sat in her carriage, and the children came from their school-rooms, and the little ones from the nursery, gathered on the front steps to greet her. In her own clear voice she gave them a few cheerful words of congratulation and counsel, while they and their caretakers listened from the veranda and front steps.

An elaborate Christmas gathering was given in 1904 in the Sanitarium gymnasium. A large Christmas tree occupied the center of the room, prettily trimmed and supplied with presents for each little member of the extensive Haskell Home family. These were generously contributed by several merchants and tradesmen interested in the success of this philanthropic undertaking.

In February, 1905, delegates of the state Y.M.C.A. Convention at the Sanitarium climbed into rigs provided and were driven to the Haskell Home for orphans, where they observed the children in the manual training and sloyd departments, dining rooms and dormitories.

Officer Hudson stopped a runaway Haskell Home team which had been frightened by the street sweeper. He was ably assisted in his rescue work by "Plum," the police dog, who took an important part in the affair, on March 29, 1905.

August 17, 1905 was "Haskell Home Day" according to Dr. Kellogg. All Sanitarium guests and patients were invited to visit the Home by taking a pleasant walk of three-quarters of a mile or ride in the four-in-hand coach. Over 100 responded to this invitation and the register at the Haskell Home showed that the visitors included representatives from Canada and twenty states of the Union. The different departments were carefully inspected, including the kitchen, sleeping apartments, laundry, class rooms, etc.

During 1906, there began rumblings within the S.D.A Church of discontent between that institution and Dr. Kellogg. The realization that they had no input over the Haskell Home led some leaders within the Church to question raising funds twice a year for something beyond their control. The schism is covered in chapter 11, but Dr. Kellogg could envision a break from their support and began his own fund-raising. The entertainment at the Sanitarium increased at this time, with proceeds going towards the Haskell Home and other local charitable organizations.

On Saturday evening, January 27, 1906, a benefit concert was provided in the Sanitarium gymnasium by the noted Roney Boys' Concert Company, for the orphans of the Haskell Home. An unusually large and enthusiastic crowd enjoyed this famous concert company.[30]

During the entertainment the boys appeared in various and picturesque costumes appropriate to the selections rendered, French court, Highland Scottish, military and patriotic uniforms added greatly to the effect produced by their voices. Tickets were available at Fisher's book store and the Sanitarium news stand. $247.80 was raised for the orphans.

About 150 ladies of the Women's League, equipped with needles, thimbles and thread, engaged in preparing garments and other material for use at Nichols Hospital and the the little inmates of Haskell Home. Work was greatly facilitated by the use of Wheeler & Wilson and Singer sewing machines, generously furnished by C. G. Eastman, agent. A social program included several numbers by the Sanitarium orchestra and an exhibition by Professor Neltons, renowned juggler and equilibrist[31].

---

[30] 1909 Poster. Invited by T. Roosevelt in 1903 to perform at the White House Children's Christmas Party for 500 guests and known throughout America and Canada. This Jubilee Anniversary celebrated twenty years of concert work by one company, with over 4,000 concerts. University of Iowa Libraries; digital.lib.uiowa.edu.

[31] One who balances himself in unnatural positions and hazardous movements. *Webster's Seventh New Collegiate Dictionary*, 1967.

A stereopticon[32] lecture in the Sanitarium gymnasium was given March 10, 1906, by Dr. W. C. Gates, formerly connected with the Calumet and Hecla Mining Company. Images were of scenery inside and outside the copper mines in the Upper Peninsula of Michigan. The admission was 15¢ for children under twelve  and 25¢ for adults. Sixteen dollars was collected to benefit the orphans of the Haskell Home.

Two weeks later, another fine stereopticon lecture was presented with views and moving pictures of "The Natural and Industrial Niagara Falls." This was presented at no charge, with a free will collection for the orphans at the Haskell Home. The program was given under the auspices of the Board of Trade of Niagara Falls, designed to stimulate an interest in the Niagara Frontier, and to show the remarkable growth and development of that district since the establishment of the large power houses. The lecture was profusely illustrated with beautifully colored lantern slides and a number of moving pictures. Forty dollars was collected for the Haskell Home.

The John Robinson Big Show came to town in May, 1906, and the circus set up in the Post second addition housed in ten acres of canvas. The parade that began at 10 A.M. was two miles in length, led by an English trap, followed by fifty cages of animals, elephants, camels, water buffaloes, Indians and U.S. Cavalrymen performing as they passed.

The big circus tent seated 20,000 and contained sensational acts, including the McNutts, in their thrilling ride in the revolving globe of death, and the Courzons, suspended high

---

[32] A double magic-lantern, by means of which the one picture appears to dissolve gradually into the other. Chamber's *Twentieth Century Dictionary*, 1904. Photo: *Wikipedia.org*.

in the air by their teeth on a tiny thread. It was a clean, honest, moral exhibition. The Haskell Home orphans were the guests of Governor Robinson at the afternoon show and enjoyed the treat immensely.

June 7, 1906 brought the severest rain, electrical and wind storm of the year. While the storm was at its height, the Haskell Home was struck by a bolt of lightning, resulting in the loss of some shingles on the cupola. A ball of fire also entered the upper portion of the building and considerable plaster was torn from the walls. No one was injured at that institution.

July 28, 1906 brought another stereopticon and phonograph entertainment at the Sanitarium gymnasium by Dr. J. Perry Worden, professor of Modern Languages at Kalamazoo College, for the benefit of the orphans of the Haskell Home. A tour of the monuments of architecture, the cities of Holland, Belgium, Germany and France, and their people, along with their choicest lyrics, ballads, songs, and national anthems, of. Admission was 15¢ and 25¢.

On Thursday, August 2, 1906, about 15 young girls from the Haskell Home left for Goguac Lake with well filled baskets. Games and other pastimes were engaged in until the noon hour, when the baskets were opened and each child did justice to their share of the luncheon. They left the lake about 5 o'clock.

H. Ruthven
MacDonald

Toronto's
Favorite
Basso-
Cantante

University of Iowa Libraries | digital.lib.uiowa.edu/tc

Miss Evangeline Smith, of this city, had on several occasions delighted large audiences at the Sanitarium with her violin. She was trained at the Conservatory of Music in Detroit. On the evening of Tuesday, September 4, 1906, Miss Smith gave a recital in the Sanitarium gymnasium, with H. Ruthven

MacDonald[33], the famous baritone soloist from Toronto, singing. The singer's fine enunciation, well-sustained tones and full, responsive voice of great range was a rare treat. Mr. MacDonald rendered double encores in response to the well deserved recalls. Mr. George Machemer was the pianist. Admission was 25¢ and 50¢, with part of the receipts going to the Haskell Home.

Scenes of "Life in the Holy Land" was performed in the Sanitarium gymnasium on Saturday evening, September 15, 1906. It was given under the direction of Miss Florence Ben-Oliel, a Christian Jewess, of Jerusalem, with twenty Sanitarium guests in genuine Palestine costume. Admission was 25¢, with net proceeds donated to the Haskell Home.

On November 10, 1906, music loving people of Battle Creek were delighted by the personnel of the Leonora Jackson Company, appearing at the Sanitarium. Miss Jackson had returned to America after three years' absence in Europe, where Queen Victoria decorated her with the Victoria Star, and the Prussian government awarded her the Mendelssohn State Prize at Berlin. She was one of the world's most noted violin artists.

Charles Edward Clarke studied for six years at the Toronto Conservatory of Music, and after touring for two years in the United States, spent several months studying in London and Paris, improving his fine and well-cultivated baritone voice.

Also on the bill was Miss Florence Marion Pace, one of Chicago's most gifted sopranos, and Ralph E. Plumer, pianist. The entertainment was for the benefit of the Haskell Home.

The Woman's League convened at the League rooms the afternoon of November 21, 1906 in spite of the unfavorable weather. They were all asked to bring their own needle, thimble and thread to sew for the Nichols Hospital, the Womans' Hospital and the Haskell Home. C. G. Eastman,

---

[33] Photo: University of Iowa Digital Library.

representing the White sewing machine, very generously donated four machines for the ladies to use. On account of the unfortunate condition caused by the weather, sewing was difficult due to the darkness, so all that was planned was not accomplished, but the ladies expected to finish their work the first part of December, as it was greatly needed.

The "Roney's Boys" Concert Company returned for a Christmas concert Saturday evening, December 22, 1906. Tickets were 25¢ and 50¢, children under fifteen years, 15¢, the net proceeds going to the Haskell Home.

On News Years Day, 1907, there was a Grand Indian Pow Wow, with games, drills and races, in the Sanitarium gymnasium. Indians in costume with feathers, paint, and war-whoops. Admission for reserved seating 35¢, general admission 25¢ and children under 15 years, 15¢, with net proceeds benefiting the orphans at the Haskell Home.

In January of 1907 there were two stereopticon lectures by Prof. George Wharton James,[34] author, explorer and

lecturer, held in the Sanitarium gymnasium. Saturday evening, January 12, was "Grand Canyon of the Colorado" and Monday evening, January 15, "The Famous Salton Sea." The recent message of President Roosevelt urging prompt action for the Salton Sea on the part of Congress, made the subject one of special interest. Mr. James was one of the first white men to enter the upper canyon of the Colorado. Reserved seats including both lectures, 50¢. Reserved seat, for either lecture, 35¢; general admission, 25¢, children under 14 years, 15¢. Tickets were sold at the Sanitarium Book Stand and Peet's

[34] Photo: https://en.wikipedia.org/wiki/George_Wharton_James

Central Drug Store, with the net proceeds for the orphans at the Haskell Home.

January 29, 1907 was another "Haskell Home Day." Sanitarium guests and patients were taken to the Home in sleighs. After touring the Home, they were served grape juice by the orphans.

Dr. Edward Burton McDowell, lecturer, traveler, correspondent, of Chicago gave a lecture on "The Panama Canal" Saturday afternoon, February 2, 1907. The talk was illustrated by stereopticon lantern slides and moving pictures at the Sanitarium gymnasium. This was another benefit for the Haskell Home.

A large audience greeted H. Ruthven MacDonald's return, the noted baritone, at the Sanitarium February 20, 1907, and a neat sum was cleared for the benefit of the Haskell Home. He won the applause of the audience from the time he sang his first number until the close of the program. Mrs. MacDonald accompanied him throughout on the piano. The musical program was interspersed with two readings, "The Fisherman's Story" and "Me and Jim," which Mr. MacDonald gave himself, proving that he was a most capable entertainer.

John B. Ratto, the renowned impersonator and humorist, performed in the Sanitarium gymnasium on February 26, 1907, for the benefit of the Haskell Home. Each part of his performance was built on the previous act, making a grand panorama of associated characters. He did his own makeup in full view of his audience, telling an appropriate story all the while. When finished he turned quickly to surprise everyone with the

accuracy of his presentation. Admission 15¢, 25¢ and 35¢.[35]

The Cleveland Ladies Orchestra, whose charming music had been heard by hundreds of Battle Creek citizens, appeared at the Sanitarium Saturday evening, March 9, 1907. Reserved seat diagram was available at Peet's Central Drug store. Tickets were 25¢ and 50¢ to benefit the orphans at the Haskell Home.

Prof. L. R. Taft, of the Agricultural college, inspector of orchards, informed West End farmers that T. A. Farrand would be in Battle Creek on Monday, March 25, 1907, to give a demonstration of spraying in the orchard at the Haskell Home. Mr. Farrand recently gave the demonstration in the orchard of W. R. Wooden, but that exhibition was on a Saturday and the Seventh Day Adventists' could not be present, so this date would accommodate the West End people and all other persons interested were invited. Recently Mr. Gibson was obliged to cut down four plum trees, ten pear trees and 54 peach trees, killed by the San Jose scale.[36] This was only one of many orchards ruined in the vicinity of Battle Creek. By attending this demonstration everyone learned how to make and apply the lime and sulphur mixture. Harry Hill of Lake Goguac secured a pump and outfit for spraying and was so overwhelmed with orders from people who want their orchards sprayed that he could not accommodate them all.

An interesting stereopticon lecture was given in the Sanitarium gymnasium on Saturday evening, March 30, 1907, by Prof. J. Perry Worden, Ph.D., entitled "Touring Great Britain on Next to Nothing," profusely illustrated with original photographs in stereopticon views. Admission 25¢ and 35¢; children 15¢, benefit for the Haskell Home.

---

[35] Photo saved from *ebay.com* by T. Maginnis.

[36] The San Jose scale is a hemipterous insect, an agricultural pest as it causes damage and crop losses to many fruit crops. It derives its popular name from San Jose, California where it was discovered and named in 1881. It was considered the most pernicious scale insect in the United States.

Prof. Allen H. Carpenter, headmaster of Kenilworth College School, gave an illustrated lecture, with stereopticon views on the "Passion Play," in the Sanitarium gymnasium, Wednesday evening, April 3, 1907. Admission 25¢ and 35¢; children, 15¢, benefit for the Haskell Home.

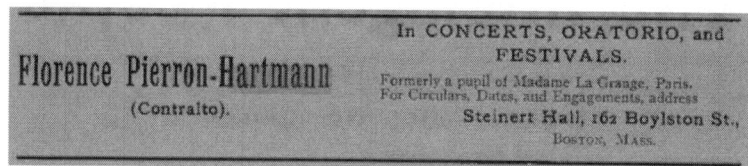

Florence Pierron-Hartmann
(Contralto).

In CONCERTS, ORATORIO, and FESTIVALS.
Formerly a pupil of Madame La Grange, Paris.
For Circulars, Dates, and Engagements, address
Steinert Hall, 162 Boylston St.,
Boston, Mass.

Mrs. Florence Perron-Hartmann, mezzo-soprano, gave a recital in the Sanitarium gymnasium, Tuesday evening, April 9, 1907. Her repertoire was varied and classical, and included a number of French songs. Tickets were on sale at the Sanitarium bookstand, to benefit the Haskell Home.

Mr. Edward Brigham, basso profundo and dramatic reader, furnished entertainment in the gymnasium for the benefit of the Haskell Home on Saturday evening, April 20, 1907.

Moving pictures furnished by Laemmie Film service of Chicago were exhibited in the Sanitarium gymnasium Saturday evening, May 4, 1907. Admission 10¢. Net proceeds were for the Haskell Home.

On Tuesday evening, May 14, 1907, the Dunbar Male Quartet and Bell Ringers entertained at the Sanitarium to benefit the Haskell Home.

Prof. J. Perry Worden gave another lecture in the Sanitarium gymnasium on Saturday evening, May 25, 1907. The subject was "Austria-Hungary and the Tyrol Mountains." Proceeds went to the Haskell Home.

Clarence Bird, the famous pianist performed at the Battle Creek Sanitarium for one hour, Tuesday evening, June 4, 1907. A diagram of reserved seats and tickets were available at Peet's Drug store. Benefit for the Haskell Home.

The famous Danish pianist, Marie Schade[37], gave a concert at the Sanitarium, Wednesday evening on June 12, 1907 to benefit the Haskell Home. Reserved seat tickets were available at Peet's Central Drug store.

The Grand Pow-wow by the Waupakisco Tribe of the Seton Indian Nation was performed on the Sixteenth Sun of the Thunder Moon, in the Sanitarium gymnasium, on Tuesday evening, July 16, 1907. Admission 20¢. There were a limited number of reserved seats, 35¢. Children under 14 years of age, 10¢. The proceeds went to benefit the Haskell Home.

The Haskell Home children were given a picnic at the Sanitarium Villa Goguac, Monday afternoon, July 29, 1907.

H. Ruthven MacDonald, Canada's famous baritone, assisted by Miss Evengeline Smith, violinist, gave a concert at the Sanitarium, Tuesday evening, July 30, 1907.

On Saturday afternoon, November 22, 1908, the children of the Haskell Home were taken out for a drive around the city. The little folks thoroughly enjoyed the trip.

A benefit basketball game – the stenographers and women nurses' indoor baseball teams of the Sanitarium made

---

[37] Marie Schade was a Danish pianist who performed with the Berlin Philharmonic. She later taught at a public school near St. Louis, Missouri. Photo courtesy of Philip Hale Photograph Collection, Boston Public Library, Massachusetts.

plans to be played. The funds obtained went toward a Christmas present fund for the children of the Haskell Home.

The children of the Haskell Home were entertained Christmas Eve at the Sanitarium gymnasium, which was decorated with evergreen, red bells and streamers. In the east end, a large fireplace was built with a burning gas log, providing warmth and comfort for the happy little ones. Over the glowing coals hung three immense stockings. On each side of the fireplace stood a mammoth Christmas tree glittering with bright lights and tinsel. The program began with a Christmas song by the children of the Haskell Home, followed by songs and recitations by the children and others.

After the program, gifts were distributed, each child receiving something practical, a toy and a sack containing a popcorn ball, an orange, candy and nuts. Every little girl from seven to eleven was made happy with a doll, the older girls receiving beauty pins, books or hair ribbons. The boys were delighted with miscellaneous toys, jack-knives, saws, balls, etc. Among the useful gifts were suits, shirts, mittens, gloves, caps for boys and girls, ties, suspenders, in fact everything to add to their comfort and happiness. The business men of the city had very liberally donated these garments and gifts. Sanitarium nurses, patients and some outside friends kindly dressed the dolls, all of them being very prettily attired.

From the gymnasium the children were taken to the dining room where refreshments were served at five o'clock. The happy little ones were then sent to their respective homes, many of them having had the merriest times of their lives. Those living at a distance were given street car tickets that they might end the joyful occasion with a ride.

The management of the Sanitarium booked Miss Clara Langhorne Clemmens[38] for the evening of January 9, 1909. Miss Clemens, daughter of the famous humorist Samuel Clemmens (Mark Twain), was assisted by Marie Nichols, violinist, who gave a recital in the gymnasium. The two artists had just returned from a very successful tour of Europe that was spoken of very highly by the foreign press. The proceeds of the entertainment were donated to the Haskell Home.

On June 29, 1910, the Haskell Home Sunday School joined over a dozen other Sunday Schools for a picnic at Willard Park, Goguac Lake. More than 1,200 children enjoyed the noon day feast, followed by songs and an address by Prof. F. S. Goodrich of Albion College. There were games, contests, hunts, athletic sports and in the afternoon a group picture was taken.

On October 15, 1910, a large crowd at the Sanitarium were entertained by Miss Harriett Williams, a reader from Chicago, assisted by Miss Mary Ross, soprano. The purpose was a benefit to raise money to buy library books for the Haskell Home children. The little ones had been without their library since the fire destroyed the main building[39].

One hundred poor children, and fifty inmates of the Haskell Home all participated in the 1911 Christmas entertainment at the Sanitarium chapel. A thousand foot reel of "Mother Goose" moving pictures was presented. There was no Christmas tree, but baskets of food and presents for each child were supplied.

---

[38] Photo: en.wikipedia.org/wiki/Clara_Clemens
[39] See Chapter 12 for the 1909 Haskell Home Fire.

The girls of the Fellowship Club of the Y.W.C.A. went to the Haskell Home, Tuesday, Feb. 6, 1912, to give the children an hour or two of enjoyment. They brought candy and games to amuse the children. They planned to leave the interurban station at 6:30.

The children of the Haskell Home had a big Christmas tree in 1913, and also were given presents. The money was raised by subscription. At noon they enjoyed a delicious Christmas dinner.

Misses Hoodner and Nida provided entertainment at the Haskell Home Halloween party, October 31, 1914.

The children of the Haskell Home deprived themselves of the childish joys that ten cents would purchase in order to add that sum to the Belgian flour contribution in December of 1914. After the children contributed their gift at the Sanitarium Sabbath School, the teachers contributed an additional sum, making the total equivalent to the price of a barrel of flour. This barrel will be sent to the desolate Belgians.

Edward H. Wood, an expert swimmer from Brooklyn, New York, was the headliner at an aquatic exhibition given December 22, 1914, in the Sanitarium women's indoor pool. The routines included swimming, diving and feature stunts in the water. The $16.30 cleared was turned over the the Haskell Home for the benefit of the children of that institution.

Christmas morning in 1914 the children at the Haskell Home enjoyed a Christmas tree filled with toys and gifts for the pleasure of the little folks. The tree was provided by Dr. J. H. Kellogg and the nurses at the Sanitarium, and Santa Claus distributed the gifts.

A meeting of the Sanitarium Nurses Alumni association was held at the Haskell Home during the third week of February, 1915. The members did some mending for the children.

A unique feature of the Local Option Workers'[40] banquet at the Sanitarium annex held in March, 1916, was the appearance of fifty children from the Haskell Home who marched through the dining room. Supporting the temperance movement, each child carried a closed umbrella, signifying that the community was "dry."

In February, 1915, Miss Bessie Ladd conducted piano lessons for eight children from the Haskell Home who would otherwise grow up without this advantage. The class, composed of five boys and three girls were given according to the Fletcher method, which embodied the modern kindergarten idea as applied to music. Miss Ladd conducted these lessons without remuneration. When the lessons first started, they were held at the Haskell Home where the children had the use of two pianos. Later, the children went to her studio in the Annex block on South Jefferson Avenue, and Professor John Martin's music studio.

Seven older boys had a pleasant outing July 25, 1918, when S. H. Small took them to the circus, where they saw everything, including the big show. Many of them had never seen a circus before.

These entertainers highlighted in this chapter came to Battle Creek specifically for the enjoyment of the orphans or to raise funds for their benefit. There were many other world-class performers that performed at the San for the pleasure of those residents and guests.

---

[40] A phrase first used by Mr. Gladstone in a letter in 1868 for the determination by vote of the people of a town or district as to whether licenses to sell intoxicating liquors shall be granted or not. Chamber's *Twentieth Century Dictionary*, 1904.

Chapter 8.

The challenge of gathering children of all ages from destitute homes and introducing these waifs to education, faith, etiquette and basic manners was an admirable goal. In reality, complete success can be a moving target that is out of reach. Many children welcomed this new family that cared for them, while others resented their removal of the only world they knew. These are a few stories of the inmates and other delinquent activities that involved the Haskell Home neighborhood.

On Sunday, June 26, 1899, Fred Underhill found a young lad wandering around the streets near the Advance Thresher shops, bare-headed, bare-footed and in a weak condition from hunger. He took the child to the police station where it was found that he belonged at the Haskell Home and had been away from that institution for over a day, having slept at some person's house on the south side and left that morning. The boy gave his name as Virgil Stockford, aged nine years.[41]

On April 27, 1900, Miss Blanche Turner, aged 13, was arrested by Constable Smith for incorrigibility. The complaint filed by Superintendent Cummings, of the Haskell Home. She was arraigned before Justice Rowell and sentenced to the school for girls at Adrian until her twenty-first birthday.

July 11, 1900, Clay Elston (10) Alabama, Fred Grueer (10) Texas, and Willis Gillis (12) of Chicago, inmates of the Haskell Home, took a horse and open buggy from the Home and drove around town buying various articles with money taken from Miss Fakin, of that Home.

While not directly related to inmates, an article in the July 23, 1900 *Battle Creek Moon*, tells of Lloyd Webster who came to town with his horse and cart and left his horse unattended by

---

[41] Found on the 1900 census at the Haskell Memorial Home, born Nov. 1890. He died April 29, 1909 and was buried in Pinconning, Michigan.

the roadside. About one o'clock Sunday morning he went to sleep at the dormitory of the Haskell Home laundry. He was apprehended by Mrs. Cummings, the manager of that institution, who turned him over to the police. Patrolman Burt found the horse and cart over on Washington Avenue South, and took it in charge. Mr. Webster was arraigned before Recorder Hamm the next morning and fined $4.80.

There was some excitement at the Home in November, 1900, when Burdett Flint of Bedford left his rig in front of the Haskell Home while he went in to see a child whom he intended to adopt. While he was gone, his horse took fright at a piece of paper blown about the road, and started at a run. When approaching Van Buren Street, the animal ran close to a tree and the vehicle caught and held fast. The harness gave way, and the animal continued his panicked race to Flint's house. Every wheel of the carriage was demolished. There was no mention of any outcome of the intended adoption.

In January, 1901, Frank Gould left his two children at the Haskell Home, agreeing to pay a certain amount per month for their board in advance. He went away assuring the staff that he would return the next day and pay for the first month, but he did not return. One of his children was seriously ill, and they were very anxious to contact Mr. Gould. The staff were willing to keep the children if they could obtain legal control of them.

Around the month of August, 1903, Mr. and Mrs. H. H. Cheetam adopted twelve-year-old Rosa Wheeler and took her home from the orphanage. On the afternoon of May 3, 1904, Mrs. Cheetam and the little girl left their house on Harris Avenue and went to the home of Mrs. Cheetam's Mother, Mrs. Fannie Wood, 54 Hazel Street. "Russie was given permission to go to the Haskell Home, where she was a ward and from that time until 3:30 the next afternoon we have not seen her. She had several times before caused us a great deal of worry and had not returned home at the time she was told to, but never stayed away all night before.

"She was dressed in a grey dress, white apron, wore no hat and has a bright and light complexion."

The matron of the Haskell Home was interviewed and stated that a part of the family of that institution left early yesterday afternoon for a walk in the country. Rosa accompanied them and seemed much pleased with the opportunity to be with her former playmates again. About 7:00 P.M., Rosa left the Home and said that she was going home. All efforts to locate her upon the part of her parents, County Agent Whitey and Chief Farrington were fruitless.

Nearly a week later, Rosa was arraigned before Justice Merrit on a juvenile disorderly charge, preferred by Mrs. Cheetam. It seems that the girl was incorrigible and had no idea of responsibility. She ran away at all chances, and even at her young age she was regarded as too much for the ordinary family to keep in control. She was committed to the Adrian school by Justice Merritt, on the recommendation of County Agent Whitney.

Patrolman Hudson stopped Lewis Foster, Willie Baird and Paul Robie, aged 6, 7 and 8 years respectively, the evening of September 27, 1905. After a short conversation, he learned that they were inmates of the Haskell Home, and desired to reach some relatives who lived in Syracuse, New York. They were prevailed upon to return to the Home and promised not to run away again.

Bicycle thefts throughout the summer of 1907 were solved when W. R. French reported his wheel stolen from the curb at the side of the Tabernacle, while he was inside attending the Purity Conference. James Armstrong, a twelve year old boy was found riding it on West Main Street. He was arrested, charged with larceny and locked up at police headquarters. Armstrong said he and a couple of other boys, Guy Coutant, aged 13 and Howard Labago, about 15, were equally guilty in various bicycle disappearances. A lad rooming in the Peterson block, West Main Street, was also implicated and made a confession of stealing a couple of other bicycles.   Armstrong told the police that they took Mr. French's wheel to the Rathbun repair shop to have the seat lowered and the handle bars let down.   Armstrong promised that he did not want to go to the reform school and that he would never do it again.   Chief Farrington promised the youngsters another chance, with the warning that any repetitions would be referred to the county agent.   In less than two years, James Armstrong would be involved in a much more serious event.

Mrs. R. S. Owen of the Haskell Home, notified the police department the evening of July 31, 1908, that seven-year-old Orin Confer was missing from that place, since morning.   The little fellow was later found that night in the neighborhood.

Mrs. Charles Waller placed her ten-year-old son Howard in the Haskell Home in August, 1908, so that he might be properly cared for since her work kept her away from home during the daytime.   The youngster ran away from the institution and returned home several times.   She called upon the police department for assistance. Patrolman Jenkins talked with the boy and secured his promise to return to the institution and to stay there.

Constable   Fonda   was   called   Saturday   morning, November 21, 1908 to Mr. Waller's residence, where his son refused to return to the Haskell Home.   The lad readily acquiesced when the officer appeared at his home.

Frank Kelley, a resident of Washington Heights requested his wife to meet him near the Haskell Home with their two children to get some peaches.   The whole family were industriously appropriating the fruit when Mr. Owen discovered them stealing from the orphans. As he approached the family, Mr. Kelley deserted his family and ran through the bushes. When Mr. Owen overtook him, Kelley disclaimed all knowledge of the presence of his family in the peach orchard. "Better settle with him right now," the wife yelled to Kelley as the two men returned to the scene of the crime.   Mr. Kelley attempt to follow this advice, but instead Mr. Owen signed a complaint before Justice Davis and Mr. Kelley was locked up at police headquarters on the charge of larceny. He was formerly employed at the institution, working as a farm laborer. He was sentenced to thirty days in the Marshall Jail without the alternative of a fine.

On the evening of January 21, 1912, a boy carelessly threw a lighted match down the stairs at the Haskell Home, where it scorched a small amount of carpet and furniture, causing fire departments 1, 2 and 4 to respond. The fire was extinguished before their arrival with a loss of $15.

At five o'clock, on the evening of February 11, 1912, the Haskell Home was set afire for the third time. Mrs. Owen, accompanied by her husband, left the Institution to attend Divine Services at the Tabernacle and had been away less than twenty minutes when a basket of clothes in the kitchen was set afire and was burning up the side walls to the rooms above where fifty children were sleeping.

The fire was discovered by one of the younger children, the fire department was called, and all were safely cared for, except for two little ones suffering bad experiences as the result of the smoke.

Evidently, whoever planned that fire planned a more thorough job. The discovery of fires in four clothes closets by Superintendent R. S. Owen prevented one of the greatest disasters in the history of the city. Thorough investigation traced the origin to two boy who wanted to see the fire horses run. Neither boy was over seven years old and too young to be touched by the law.

In March of 1912, thirteen year old Sadie Stuart went to Haskell Home and asked to be taken in there, giving the name of Helen Kelley. The probation officer, Foy Stuart, asked to have her sent back to Adrian.

On August 7, 1912, a blaze started in the kitchen of the Haskell Home kitchen, but was confined to that room, and caused little damage. Engine company 1, 2 and 4 responded to the alarm.

Alfred Allen, eighteen years of age, was held on suspicion of starting the fire and arrested a short time afterward. He was a former inmate of the home and told several conflicting stories when first arrested. He admitted to sleeping in the barn the night of the fire, and admitted to being in the kitchen to get something to eat, but denied setting the fire. In every interview the police caught him lying several times, but couldn't catch him telling any truth that could hurt him. He was locked up for five days on a vagrancy charge and released with the understanding that he would return to his Mother's home at the Soo.

Little Eva Fox wandered away from the Haskell Home on July 16, 1913. She was about twelve years old, with a freckled face, brown hair and she talked exceptionally loud and fast.

In 1919, rowdies celebrated Halloween by causing the Haskell Home bell to break loose from its stable location and fall to the ground, by pulling too hard on the rope. The bell broke into several pieces when it hit the sidewalk and the children mourned its loss. The old bell performed the duty of calling the little tots to their meals and announcing the bed time hour.

On September 27, 1921, Abel Kitchel, nine years old, took a Ford coupe belonging to M. G. Lipscomb to visit his Grandmother, who resided in Marshall. Just before he reached the city limits, someone saw him, thought something was wrong and notified officers. The youth was brought to the city jail where he was questioned. He said he was living with an aunt and for a time was in the Haskell Home. He was turned over to juvenile authorities.

Kenneth Hodge's entry into the business world was fraught with grief. His father was dead and his Mother had a hard time supporting herself. He had been an inmate of the Haskell Home. In June, 1922, at the age of 17, he went to work for the district messenger service. His second errand was to take a package to the Sanitarium and collect $23. This he did but then he lost the money. He cried all night, and the next morning placed a lost ad at the *Enquirer and News* office, explaining the loss and that he would have to make good the money lost, but vowed to remain on the job if they would allow. As it was his first day on the job, he had no idea when his first paycheck would appear. Mrs. Blevins of North Wood Street found the money near her home, had seen the notice and was glad to return it to the owner.

Unfortunately, this was not the last time he appeared in newspaper print. Only a month later he was arrested for kidnapping the five month old child of Mrs. George Wagner from its cab in front of the Kresge Five and Ten cent store. Cries of women who witnessed the abduction attracted the attention of Officer Rathman, on duty at the time in the traffic booth, who gave chase to Hodge, catching him at the corner at Jackson and McCamly, just behind the Post Tavern. When questioned by Detective Hessmer, the Hodge boy said he took the child "because there was no one to watch it." The Mother was in the store at the time.

Kenneth's Mother revealed that since he was a youngster able to walk he had an abnormal love for dolls, babies, and baby clothing and doll clothing and caps. He was diagnosed with an affliction of dementia praecox[42], an increase love of babies and things associated with them until it became a mania. His room at home was always full of dolls and baby clothes which he used to pick up around the streets. For a time he stayed at the Haskell Home and later at the Starr Commonwealth near Albion. As his affliction grew he was sent to the state hospital in Kalamazoo, but his Mother succeeded in securing his release from the institution the previous year.

---

[42] The term was gradually replaced by "schizophrenia" which remains in current diagnostic use. en.wikipedia.org/wiki/Dementia_praecox.

If there was a trophy for delinquency, Jeremiah Posey would be the easy winner. With headlines of "JERRY" IN AGAIN, and CHAMPION INMATE OF CALHOUN COUNTY JAIL, his offenses included vagrancy, catching freight trains, petty larceny and escalated to malicious destruction of property, resisting arrest, fighting and drunkenness. Local newspapers relied on increased circulation whenever "Jerry" was headlined. On June 19, 1910 the *Battle Creek Sunday Journal* stated that he had spent exactly 500 out of the previous 730 days in the county jail in Marshall, Michigan. On June 20, 1910, the *Battle Creek Journal* noted he was re-arrested and sentenced to 90 days more, making his new record 590 out of 820 days. By 1912 his title was the most arrested man in the state of Michigan. The story at the precinct was that Jeremiah had been arrested more times than "John Doe." His partial police record was:

Sep. 30, 1905	Runaway, turned up October 2, 1905. Had been an inmate of the Haskell Home but would not stay there.
Dec. 10, 1905	Burglary, broke into Erney West's barn and stole a fur lap robe. Age about 14, sent to Lansing Industrial[43] school.
July 26, 1907	Vagrancy, $5.00 or 10 days. Paid. Had just returned from Lansing.
May 18, 1908	Disorderly, sentence suspended for 30 days. Became enraged at employees of the *Battle Creek Daily Journal*. He made dire threats and used profane language.
June 6, 1908	Drunk, let go on own recognizance.
June 23, 1908	Disorderly, case dismissed. Making a nuisance of himself in Monument Park.

---

[43] Referred to as the Reformatory at Lansing in other articles.

July 18, 1908	Larceny "Petit," 50 days at Marshall. Stole type metal at the *Battle Creek Daily Journal*.
Sep. 28, 1908	Drunk, $7.50 or 15 days at Marshall, committed.
Nov. 16, 1908	Larceny, "Petit," 45 days at Marshall Jail. Stole copper boilers.
May 26, 1909	Vagrancy, 45 days at Marshall[44].
June 6, 1909	Vagrancy, 45 days at Marshall.
July 27, 1909	Drunk, $7.50 or 20 days, committed.
Aug. 22, 1909	Disorderly in Monument Square Park.
Sep. 27, 1909	Disorderly, $25.00 or 60 days, committed. Fighting.
Oct. 22, 1909	Malicious destruction of property, 75 days in Marshall Jail. Broke windows at Diamond Club.[45]
Feb. 19, 1910	Drunk, 25 days in Marshall.
March 20, 1910	Indecent language, 70 days at Marshall.
May 31, 1910	Stealing ride on railway train, $8.80 or 15 days, committed.

In an interview in the *Sunday Record*, July 28, 1907, "Jerry" was born between 1890 and 1892 in Chattanooga, Tennessee.[46] Jim Posey, an Italian, was his father; Laura Posey, his Mother, was a French Creole, and Jerry didn't know what that made him.[47] Both parents died when he was so young that he couldn't remember their faces. He was sent to

---

[44] Jerry had been absent from jail for several months claiming to have spent the winter in New York. When asked why he came back the youngster answered "To get in jail, I guess."

[45] "Well, I'm sure of a Christmas dinner anyway," remarked Jerry when the sentence was passed.

[46] According to the 1910 Census [Calhoun County Jail, Marshall], his birth place was Alabama, age 19.

[47] William Taylor had a wife, Laura and step-son Jerry Posey in the 1900 census, living in North Birmingham, AL.

Mrs. Steele, an Adventist woman in Chattanooga who brought him to the Haskell Home. He lived in the Home until he was about 14, when he felt a desire to see the world outside the orphanage.

He came into the city and was given a place to sleep and something to eat at the rate of 50 cents per week. He got a job at the Advance Thresher works where he worked in the tool office. By running errands for tips from other employees, he derived an income of about $1.50 a week. When the local authorities found out that he should be in school, Jerry said he couldn't eat and sleep and go to school, because he had to have money to live, so he was sent to the reformatory.

Articles in the November 3, 1910 newspapers stated that Jerry escaped from the county jail. When sent out to rake the lawn, unguarded, Jerry failed to return for his meals, and joined the United States Army. This kept him out of the newspapers until November 8, 1911 when officers were summoned to the East Main Street Hack & Bus office to subdue Jerry who had been drinking and using profane and offensive language to women passing by. It was thought that after a short time in the service, he deserted and was dishonorably discharged. The army officials were notified but they replied that they preferred to have Battle Creek keep him. He was sentenced to sixty-five days in the Marshall Jail.

He continued to be in and out of jail (mostly in) until 1912 when he was arrested in Kalamazoo, on a charge of stealing a suitcase from the Michigan Central baggage room, containing six very expensive ladies' coats, valued at eighty dollars. This larceny charge resulted in a sentence of from two to ten years imprisonment at Jackson prison, with a recommendation of five years.[48]

He returned and was sentenced twenty days in the county jail on a disorderly charge September 10, 1917. When he was one of 120 men called for examination in the army in October

---

[48] These coats were entered as exhibits but could not be located at the circuit court evidence room when called for after the trial was over.

and in December he was sought by the federal government on the charge of being a slacker. Constable F. D. Smoke took him out to Camp Custer December 7, 1917 where he joined the army in the field artillery. He was assigned to battery 118. Less than one month later, Jerry was arraigned on a charge of burglary from E. G. Clark Coal and Wood office, stealing $23.01 from the safe in that office. He was sentenced to serve from three to seven years, with the recommendation of five years, in Jackson, for carrying a concealed weapon and as a habitual criminal. He must have only served three years, as he was taken into custody November 1, 1921, charged with violating the terms of his parole from the state prison at Jackson. Police allege that he stole a quantity of groceries from two downtown stores and was returned to the state institution.

Jeremiah Posey was arrested in May 1923 after a fight with Police Sergeant James Elliott in the rear of the post office and was arraigned on a charge of larceny of a coat and robe from an automobile on North Jefferson Avenue. He pleaded innocent, not remembering anything that transpired because he was drunk at the time on denatured alcohol. Judge Carl Gray released him without fine or jail sentence if he would return at once to South Bend, where he claimed to have a job as a cook in a restaurant. He was released from custody, but never left town.

"Jerry" started a sentence of 90 days in the county jail, as a result of a fight in which he engaged with three others on Sycamore Street in June 1923. The fight was in full battle when Detectives Bibbins and Voorhees rushed to Sycamore Street in an attempt to stop the fracas. Bibbins knocked out Posey for about 30 minutes with one punch. The others were released on bond, paid $14.40 in fines or got time with Jerry.

October 18, 1923, Jerry pleaded guilty to larceny (theft of an overcoat from the automobile of John Lockridge, parked on West Jackson Street) and sentenced to spend 65 days in the county jail. It was estimated at this time that "Jerry" had spent about one-third of his short life behind bars.

This latest arrest began when Officer Paul Keagle charged him with being drunk. As he was being led to the police station Mr. Lockridge approached the officer and told him that Posey was wearing his overcoat which had been stolen from his automobile.

Patrolman Tait then remembered seeing Posey with several blankets earlier in the evening and he also remembered that Posey had disappeared in an alley on West Jackson Street with his load. The patrolman searched the alley and found four blankets and a raincoat.

A further investigation by the police revealed Posey's cache, where police found automobile tires, rims and other accessories, believed to have been stolen from parked automobiles in the city. Citizens were invited by Chief of Police Fonda to visit the city jail and look over the articles.

While Jerry was residing at his second home at the Marshall Jail, Sheriff George W. Colby commented on his most famous inmate. Beyond his arrest record, he was also becoming as well known for his harmonizing, which was getting better every day. "You'd be surprised the number of people who come to the jail house and ask to hear Jerry sing. Some of the best people in Marshall have deserted the movies at times to come over and enjoy the concert."

He was released a few days before Christmas with new clothes, a pocket full of change and tobacco.

At 2:05 Christmas morning 1923, officers responded to a call from the Post Tavern garage of a colored man that had held up Matt Ryan near Murphy's lunch-room at South Jefferson Avenue and Jackson Street, taking twenty dollars. The officers later learned that the attempt was made by Jeremiah Posey, released from the Marshall Jail after serving a 60-day sentence, three days before. He was not found until December 29, when he was arrested on a charge of public drunkenness.

While awaiting sentencing, Jerry was arrested January 3, 1924 in possession of several stolen articles identified as having been taken from the home of Bert Johnson when it was burglarized.

Jerry's arrest occurred at the corner of Elm and East Van Burren Streets after he had entered two homes and had made another attempt to steal an automobile. The officers searched the neighborhood and caught sight of Posey as he ran across the intersection of Elm and Van Buren Streets. He was arrested after a short chase.

Posey had in his possession a dark blue overcoat, gray neck-scarf, gray hat and other articles which were later identified as the loot stolen from the home.

The headline "Jeremiah Posey Back Home" began 1924 with the statistic that he spent 250 days of the previous year in the county jail. There was the possibility discussed that the burglary charge might be changed to a charge of habitual criminal which carries with it life imprisonment. The case was continued until the March term of circuit court.

On January 28, 1924, Posey was sentenced to a term of from six months to fifteen years in Jackson prison. The judge recommended a term of one year.

He may have been imprisoned for longer than just one year, as the next mention of Jerry was in the January 1 edition of the Battle Creek Moon Journal giving Jerry Posey the distinction of being the last arrest of 1934. He was booked on a charge of intoxication and desirous of fighting every passerby along Southwest Capital Avenue.

In July 1935, he was taken into custody with two others on disorderly charges, arrested at Liberty and South McCamly Streets. This time Posey's collie dog followed and, after being thrown out several times, kept vigil outside police headquarters. In August police were summoned where Jerry and another man were arguing over ownership of a bread box filled with dishes. Both claimed the dishes belonged to them. Officers explained that the situation was a matter to be determined by civil court proceedings, and this time Jerry was not arrested.

Before the year was over, Jerry was in the city jail charged with the theft of about 500 pounds of coal. Officers saw him carrying some 50 pounds of coal in a sack. Under questioning, Posey at first said he borrowed the fuel from the home of a friend. Going to that address the officers failed to find anyone at home. In Posey's house the police found about a quarter ton of coal. He was released several days later when the police were unable to determine from which coal yard the fuel had been taken. Another few days found Jerry arrested on drunkenness charges and faced the prospect of spending Christmas in the county jail at Marshall unless he could raise the $5 fine.

January 2, 1935 found Jerry in the newspaper again, this time when the civil servants came to his rescue. Damage of $10 was caused in a blaze at his residence when a bed placed too close to a stove ignited. Two chemical tanks were used by the firemen in quenching the blaze.

No longer on Clyde Street, Jerry lived in a shack on the Hamblin Avenue dump in September of 1937. Police were informed that Posey was seen with a quantity of marijuana. In his shack they found a cigar box half full of dried marijuana. He was detained in the city jail. He pleaded guilty to charges of possession and sentenced to serve from three to four years to be served in Southern Michigan prison at Jackson.

Jerry was again in police custody on April 8, 1942 on charges of possessing narcotics. He pleaded his own case and won dismissal of the charge. It was an important victory for the defendant, for he would have faced a possible life term as a four-time offender, but by this time he had more experience in a courtroom than the most experienced prosecutor in Michigan.

In May, Posey was arraigned again, this time charged with being in possession of a loaded firearm while under the influence of liquor. The gun, a .22 caliber rifle had been stolen from a home on Lafayette Avenue with four loaded cartridges in the gun. Posey pleaded guilty and received a straight 30-day jail sentence.

In July, Jerry was digging for fish worms in a field off South Washington Avenue between the Michigan Central and Grand Trunk tracks and came across nine bundles of tractor wheel lugs, six bags of tractor parts and five cartons of grease guns hidden in tall grass near the tracks, having an estimated value of over $100. He dutifully notified the authorities. It was found that the articles had been stolen from a flat car on which six McCormic-Deering tractors were being shipped and which was handled by the Michigan Central. City police, special officers for the Duplex Printing Press Co., and detectives employed by both the Grand Trunk and Michigan Central participated in the investigation.

He was back in trouble again at the beginning of 1944, when he was apprehended on South Kendall Street after Fort Custer MPs found him carrying a .32 automatic. He was sent back to the Southern Michigan prison on a new four to five-year sentence. The article went on to itemize his incarceration record: a first arrest in 1907 on a charge of larceny, for which he served a year. He was sentenced to from two to five years in 1913 for larceny; three to nine years in 1918 for carrying a concealed weapon; six months to 15 years in 1924 for a breaking and entering, and from three to four years in 1937 for possessing narcotics. He also served numerous shorter sentences for minor violations.

The February 19, 1958 *Battle Creek Enquirer and News* carried his death notice with no mention of his checkered past that local residents knew so well:

Jeremiah Posey

Jeremiah Posey, about 77[49], who had been a resident of Battle Creek for many years, died of a heart attack last night. He had been living at 254 Lafayette St., and died while visiting at 230 Lafayette. Mr. Posey was born in the Philippine Islands, and came to Battle Creek as a boy.

---

[49] His age fluctuated from year to year, but the 1900 census shows his birth occurred Dec. 1890. This may be more accurate than the other dates.

The February 21, 1958 *Battle Creek Enquirer and News* carried his funeral arrangements:

POSEY, JEREMIAH. Friends may call at the Patton Funeral Home where funeral services will be Saturday at 10:00 a.m. Rev. R. R. Amos officiating. Burial in Bedford Cemetery.

His age and birth place changed in newspaper articles previously transcribed, but he may not have known these details about his own life. The U.S. Population census tracks him as follows.[50]

	AGE	BP	RACE	CENSUS LOCATION
1900	9	Alabama	B	North Birmingham, AL
1910	19	Alabama	B	Calhoun County Jail, Marshall
1920	28	Michigan	MU	Michigan State Prison, Jackson
1930	42	Philippine Is.	FIL	Michigan State Prison, Jackson
1940	50	Philippine Is.	W	Marquette State House of Correction

Photo: 1924 Prisoner Registry, State Prison of Southern Michigan, Jackson, Record Group 64-50, Volume 48, #9805, Archives of Michigan.

---

[50] His Race changed from Black to Mulatto to Philippian to White. Perhaps Philippians were treated less harshly than Negroes during his life.

None of these examples should overshadow the good work of the Haskell Home. History is full of successful adults who rose from the worst environments and others that floundered from the best of families. The inmates of the Haskell Home were removed from the woes of poverty, or worse, and were provided opportunities to enjoy a better future.

Chapter 9.

Assembling from fifty to one hundred and fifty children together, aged from infants to teenagers, and keeping them in close quarters twenty-four hours of every day was a guarantee of disease and injuries. The Haskell Home was no exception, as the following list compiled from local newspapers demonstrates.

1895

Percy Redner[51] died June 10, 1895 at the Haskell Home, aged 5 years. The funeral was held from the home, Elder McCoy officiated. The interment took place in Oak Hill cemetery.

Helen L. Whitman died June 11, 1895 at the Haskell Home, aged 37. The deceased was one of the first teachers at the home, and was highly respected and esteemed by a wide circle of friends.

Lina Redner[52] died June 19, 1895 at the Haskell Home, aged 3 years. The interment took place in Oak Hill cemetery.

1900

Floyd D. Waggner, aged 8y, 6m 20d, died at the Haskell Home Jan. 20, 1900 of acute nephritis[53]. The remains were taken to Old Burlington cemetery, Burlington, Michigan for interment.

Roy Rounds, aged 9, son of Mrs. Rhoda Rounds of Bedford drowned in St. Mary's Lake August 5, 1900. The party of about twenty children from the Haskell Home under the supervision of Miss Long and three other Mothers, were enjoying a picnic and swimming. When they walked around

---

[51] Name in obituary was Percy Reedman.

[52] Name on FindaGrave.com and obituary is Alene Reedman.

[53] Nephritis is often caused by infections, and toxins, but is most commonly caused by autoimmune disorders that affect the major organs like kidneys. Chamber's *Twentieth Century Dictionary*, 1904.

the lake to the swimming beach on the north shore of the lake, Roy waded out beyond his depth and being unable to swim, sank immediately.   His small companions were unable to realize the peril of the lad and he died without any assistance. The body was recovered after a few minutes by two men who were swimming further out in the lake when he went down.

His Mother, Mrs. Rhoda Rounds, was a widow and placed her son in the Haskell Home on April 6, 1897 where he resided until his death. Mrs. Rounds recently underwent a very delicate surgical operation at the Sanitarium Hospital and was convalescing at her home in Bedford. The funeral was held in the assembly room of the Home, and interment was made at the Haskell Home cemetery.

1901

Smallpox cases in the west end were released from quarantine on May 17, and the tents where they had been quartered near the Haskell Home were taken down.

Katy Bronson, aged 2 years, died at the Haskell Home Aug. 26, 1901, of rickets[54].   The remains were shipped by undertaker James T. Caldwell, to her parents, Eugene and Georgia Bronson, Punta Gorda, Florida, where the funeral services and interment were made.

The funeral services of Edna Grace Hopkins, the two-year-old daughter of Mrs. Hopkins were conducted Sep. 18, 1901 by Elder S. H. Lane at the Haskell Home and interment was made in Haskell Home cemetery.

1902

Clayton Huntley, age 10, died March 23, 1902, at the Haskell Home.   Consumption[55] was the cause of the lad's death.

---

[54] Rickets is a condition that results in weak or soft bones in children. Chamber's *Twentieth Century Dictionary*, 1904.

[55] Consumption, now referred to as tuberculosis is an infectious disease that generally affects the lungs.

1903

The epidemic of whooping cough eased in April. However Carrie E. Smith, aged one year, died from whooping cough October 6, 1903. Buried in the Haskell Home cemetery.

1904

About the middle of March the first case of measles came into the Home and despite every effort to prevent the disease from spreading, it was communicated to others. Twenty-three children suffered an attack of measles, and 93 others were exposed. Some of the regular caretakers were put in quarantine with their families, while others were working night and day in the discharge of their duties. Some of the cases were unusually severe and only the most heroic efforts upon the part of the physicians and nurses prevented complications which might have escalated into more serious conditions.

1905

At the opening of the year, a recently arrived member of the family entered the church school with measles and this caused an epidemic that spread to thirty-two cases. The staff did its own nursing, thus saving quite a bit of expense. Medical attendance, when needed, was provided from the Sanitarium for free.

John D. Artlip, the baby wonder at the Sanitarium, died as the result of an acute attack of gastric trouble. The baby prodigy was pronounced by physicians to be the strongest baby in the United States.

December – Eight children of the Haskell home came down with diphtheria and were at once removed to the Austin farm, thus, what might have been a serious epidemic was averted. As a precautionary measure the anti-toxin treatment was administered to every child in the home, as well as the officials and the workmen employed about the place.

1909

Feb. 5, 1909 Cecil Coutant (12), George Goodenow (10) and Lena McKelvey (14) died in a fire that destroyed the Haskell Home within two hours. All were buried at the Haskell Home Cemetery in a single coffin. More details in chapter 12.

August 13, 1909 – Donald Webber, seven months old, died from cholera infantum at the Haskell Home, the third child in Battle Creek to die from this disease in a week. Many babies around the city were ill with it.

In August, seven-years-old Frankie Lang, contracted measles during an epidemic at the orphanage. The case was unusually severe necessitating the use of a hot water bottle on the afflicted joints. Inadvertently the boy was burned on the calf of his leg so badly, that the flesh was burned almost to the bone. The heroic sacrifice made by six nurses at Nichols Hospital volunteered to each have three square inches of healthy skin cut from their flesh to graft on the little fellow's limb. The difficult operation of grafting thirty-six different pieces of skin was successful.

1911

Four children at the Haskell Home contracted scarlet fever October 5, 1911, and were isolated in another building close by. Three of the children were girls and one was a boy. The other children were attending school as the home was properly fumigated. The quarantine was lifted October 27, 1911.

1912

April 5, 1912 – Eva June Campbell, aged one year and four months, died at the Haskell Children's home, from pleural pneumonia. Buried at the Haskell Home Cemetery.

Marguerite, five-year-old daughter of Mrs. Emma J. Jones, died at the Haskell Home, where she had been a ward, the morning of June 18, 1912. Convulsions speeded the little girl's demise. The Home had a large garden where it raised food for its inmates. Strawberries being ripe, the inmates of the Home had been picking berries during their idle hours, and yesterday Margaret went out with the helpers. After some time the little girl complained to Mrs. Owen that her stomach ached. She said she had eaten many berries, and Mrs. Owen was of the opinion this was the cause of her discomfort. Consequently she left the patch, with the child hanging on to her arm, and went to the house. On the way the child stopped to vomit and was given some medicine and put to bed.

About 11 o'clock the child awoke with convulsions. Dr. W. S. Martin of the Sanitarium was called, the physician for the Haskell Home, but despite his efforts the convulsions grew worse, and shortly after one o'clock she passed away. A stomach pump was used on the child and no traces of ptomaine poisoning were found. The little girl had been sickly some time before, so it was the belief of the physician that the berry acid brought on the convulsions through poisoning of the blood. None of the other children were affected by eating the berries, although it was claimed they all gorged themselves when turned loose in the patch. Mrs. Jones had been confined to her bed with illness, and unable to take care of her children.

June 25, 1912 – Willard Kenneth Owen, the eighteen-month-old adopted son of Mr. and Mrs. R. S. Owen of the Haskell Home, died of gastritis. The funeral service was held at the Home and the interment took place the Haskell Home Cemetery.

1917

A case of chicken pox broke out at the Haskell Home and the place was quarantined April 11, 1917, by Sanitary Officer Fred Hahn.

1919

During the beginning of September, 1919, Manley Billings, aged seven years, of the Haskell Home, was ill with diphtheria. Edward McNally of 118 Marjorie Street came down with smallpox and moved from the detention hospital to the Haskell Home. "No one knows when or where the malady [smallpox] may spring up and it is always best to be on the lookout," said one of the health officials, "especially just now with the schools opening for the fall semester."

1922

Gabriel Gonzales, age nine years, died at the Sanitarium hospital, Feb. 2, 1922. He was attending the Haskell Home when his sled was coasting downhill and collided with another. He received a wound in the head which was not considered serious at first. His Mother, Mrs. Marguerite Gonzales, brought him from Mexico about four years before.

On November 8, 1922, Mrs. Elizabeth Green, Matron at the Haskell Home was ill with diphtheria and removed to the Kimball detention hospital.

These deaths, while frequent, seem to be better than the population as a whole, considering this was a household of over one hundred children for most of the years of operation. Many childhood diseases were more deadly back when there were fewer medical cures available, and knowledge of transmission was also in doubt.

According to statista.com, child mortality rates (under 5 years old) in the United States during the time of the Haskell Home operations were:

YEAR	UNDER 5
1895	25.7%
1900	23.9%
1905	22.0%
1910	20.7%
1915	18.0%
1920	18.5%
1925	13.7%

Chapter 10.

The Haskell Home Laundry
Historical Society of Battle Creek Archives

On the afternoon of April 5, 1903, shortly after one o'clock, Engineer George Harris began to repair some pipes and do a little plumbing about the engine room. The power house was a brick building, about forty by fifty feet, on the ground floor with a high basement. It was located a safe distance northwest of the main building[56]. The laundry machinery was located on the upper story where there were living apartments for the laundress.

He lighted a gasoline furnace used by plumbers and commenced melting lead. Suddenly and unexpectedly, the gasoline receptacle exploded, the burning liquid flying in every direction. Mr. Harris was completely enveloped in flames. His clothing was set on fire and burning gasoline was scattered all about the room, setting fire to the timbers and material in the room.

With his clothes on fire he rushed out of the building and rolled in the snow, thrusting his arms in the snow banks to his

---

[56] See map on back cover for location of building relative to orphanage.

shoulders to alleviate the pain and thus unaided extinguished the flames which were threatening his life. An orphan boy who was also in the engine room and received a badly burned face, ran out, crying fire and gave the alarm to the people in the main building who at once notified the fire departments and later the Police Headquarters, calling the ambulance for the injured engineer, who was tenderly placed in the patrol ambulance and driven to the West Hall of the Sanitarium for treatment. He was badly burned about the face, arms and hands by the explosion, and his hair and eye brows were nearly burnt off.

The apparatus from No. 2 station and the chief's wagon at once responded to the alarm turned in by telephone at 1:18. When the chief arrived he found a line of hose working from No. 2's apparatus, but the distance was a thousand feet in length and the water delivered was inadequate for there was only a four-inch main at this spot. He at once ordered that the engine from No. 2 be brought out and this was done though it required five horses to draw the five ton weight over the heavy roads.

The department succeeded in preventing the fire from spreading and saved a frame house and barn that were near the power house. The Home building was at no time in danger for it was located some distance from the power house, where light and heat were being transmitted to the main building through a tunnel.

The power house was gutted by the flames. It was a brick building, about forty by fifty feet in ground area. Most of the laundry machinery was destroyed and the engine and electrical apparatus in the power house were put out of commission. The Nichols & Shepard company furnished a portable boiler and traction engine to provide temporary heat for the institution and by ten o'clock that night the main building was being heated by steam from its plant again. The Advance Thresher Company also provided equipment and a large number of citizens worked to complete the temporary conversion.

The head laundress was a widow, who with her four children lived in apartments in the laundry, directly above the engine room. Fortunately no one was in those quarters during the inferno, but all their clothing and household effects were consumed in the fire. The building had an estimated loss of $3,000 but insurance held by the Hubbard agency amounted to only $1,500.

While the Battle Creek *Morning Enquirer* was advertising fine clothes for Easter – hats, shoes, suits, coats, gloves and even corsets, the children were suddenly without most of their clothes that were in the weekly washing and consumed in the fire at the laundry area, one week before Easter. More than one-half of the clothing of the 110 orphans were destroyed.

The ladies of Perfection Hive had a donation party at the Maccabee Hall on April 16, for the children at the Haskell Home. Members were encouraged to bring any clothing or bedding to the Hall. Other groups conducted sewing circles.

All summer the half-open canning shed built over the coal cellar was used for laundry work. The boilers were covered with rough boards to keep off the rain, and the rest of the building was roofless.

Ruins of the power-house and laundry
The Haskell Home Appeal, Vol. 7, No. 1, Oct. 1903

The power-house and laundry was rebuilt and after the main building was destroyed by fire in 1909, the laundry building was used as the orphans' home until 1922, although this smaller building could accommodate only about 40 children.

Chapter 11.

Mrs. Ellen White, one of the founders of the Seventh Day Adventists religion had for some time grown uneasy with all the holdings of the Church in one location, a location that was growing faster than other towns of similar size. At the biennial General Conference of the church in 1901 the College was moved to a less worldly setting, far from the sophisticated atmosphere of the San. Battle Creek College[57] went to Berrien Springs, Michigan.

Still the flock seemed to like Battle Creek more than their prophetess did.

Warnings came from Mrs. White. She had been shown in a vision a great sword, gleaming and flashing and turning. It was a sword of fire – poised over Battle Creek.[58] In the next few years, after fires destroyed the Sanitarium Health Food Co., the Battle Creek Sanitarium and the *Review and Herald* publishing building, Sister White described it as a punishment for a laggard church "The Lord is not very well pleased with Battle Creek."

After the San was destroyed by fire in 1902, Dr. Kellogg was pressured to rebuild the "San" elsewhere but promised "the noblest temple of health and healing that the sun ever shown upon," would be erected on the old site. Mrs. White moved to California and the schism grew wider as Dr. Kellogg developed his ambitious plans for an even larger Sanitarium building

Arthur G. Daniells, President of the Seventh-day Adventist General Conference found Dr. Kellogg overbearing, and difficult. Dr. Kellogg viewed the S.D.A. unreceptive to his grand plans. He also became skeptical of Ellen White's prophecies and was accused of pantheism.

Dr. Kellogg tried to remove Daniells from the General Conference Executive Committee, which failed, and then,

---

[57] Now known as Andrews University.
[58] nonsda.org/egw/egw71.shtml

Daniells rallied his own supporters at the General Conference to pass a resolution declaring that Adventist institutions must be owned by church members and administered directly through one of the agencies of the General Conference. Dr. Kellogg in turn retaliated by dissolving the International Medical Missionary and Benevolent Association in 1905, but not before transferring its assets to the sanitarium, leaving only its debts to the General Conference.[59]

The *Haskell Home Appeal* in volume IX, No. 3, April 1906, reminded its members that another special collection would take place on April 7, for the Orphans and the Aged. In the same issue appeared the following annual financial report of the Haskell Home and James White Memorial Home for 1905:

RECEIPTS

Donations from conferences and churches	$5,875.97
Donations from individuals	733.95
Total	$6,609.92
Received on board and clothing (Haskell Home)	$2,385.23
Received on board and clothing (J. White Home)	321.45
Received on legacies	770.14
Received on tuition	26.25
Received on interest (Haskell estate)	450.00
Received on *Haskell Home Appeal* subscriptions	7.73
Received from farm (cash sales and teaming)	5,650.03
	$16,220.75

---

[59] See *John Harvey Kellogg*, M.D. by Richard W. Schwarz and *Dr. John Harvey Kellogg and the Religion of Biologic Living* by Brian C. Wilson.

EXPENDITURES

Labor	$3,115.43	$860.88
Provisions	2,972.27	846.31
Light and Fuel	1,652.44	624.32
Farm	2,498.06	
Household Expenses	1,240.45	495.53
Clothing	557.29	24.28
Educational	263.88	
Medical	117.60	189.61
Insurance	60.00	
Taxes		19.24
Office supplies and postage	51.05	
Administrative	125.07	21.86
Haskell Home Appeal	163.91	
	$12,817.45	$3,082.03
	3,092.03	
Total	$15,899.48	

In 1907 Dr. Kellogg was asked by the Battle Creek Seventh-day Adventist Church to resign from the congregation, but he refused. Dr. Kellogg was disfellowshipped, and he made no effort to fight their unanimous decision. With this split, almost all denominational support for the Haskell Home and other S.D.A. projects under Dr. Kellogg's control was lost.

This was followed by the statistical Report for the institutions:

Haskell Home:

Total number of children received	606
Number of children, Jan. 1, 1905	110
Number of children received during 1905	48
Number of children placed in homes or returned to friends	56
Number of children in Haskell Home Jan. 1, 1906	102
Number of applications received during 1906	109
Number of teachers employed during school year	5
Number of caretakers and assistants	12
Number of other employees	14

James White Memorial Home:[60]

Total number of persons received	123
Number of persons Jan. 1, 1905	30
Number of persons received during 1905	48
Number of persons left during 1905	56
Number of persons died during 1905	4
Number of persons Jan. 1, 1906	33

At the Seventeenth Annual Session of the General Conference of Seventh-day Adventist, October 4, 1878, the following action was taken:

WHEREAS, The impression has gone out from some unknown cause that J. H. Kellogg, M.D., holds infidel sentiments, which does him great injustice, and also endangers his influence as physician-in-chief of the Sanitarium; therefore

WHEREAS, That in our opinion justice to the doctor and the Institute under his medical charge, demand that he should have the privilege of making his sentiments known, and that he be invited to address those assembled on this ground, upon the harmony of science and the Sacred Scriptures.

This resolution was unanimously adopted after which the Conference adjourned to the call of the chair.

Matters came to a head in April, 1907 when the Tabernacle congregation termed an attempt on the part of the Sanitarium authorities to rob them of the White Memorial Home for the aged, and the Haskell Home for orphans. Because it was felt that both institutions were hostile to the Seventh-day Adventist church by attacking the beliefs on which that religion was founded, it was felt that removal of all S.D.A. inmates from both institutions was necessary.

---

[60] Both heading were Haskell Home, but the number seems to reflect the two institutions as corrected.

The General Conference made the following propositions to the managers of these two incorporated institutions:

WHEREAS, The James White Memorial Home and the Haskell Home originally belonged to the Seventh-day Adventist Medical Missionary and Benevolent Association; therefore –

RESOLVED, that the General Conference Committee [unreadable word] the responsibility of caring for the aged people in the James White Memorial Home, according to the list supplied by the managers of the Home, at a rate of $2.50 per week for each person not otherwise provided for, beginning April 6, 1907.

RESOLVED, that the General Conference Committee provide for the Seventh-day Adventist orphan children in the Haskell Home, according to the list furnished by the managers, at the rate of $1.50 per week for each child not otherwise provided for, from April 6, 1907, while steps were being taken to provide homes elsewhere for these children.

RESOLVED, that the following persons: Elder M. N. Campbell, G. W. Amadon, A. L. Bayley, constitute a local correspondence bureau, corresponding with union and local conference organizations and individuals, in finding homes for inmates of these institutions.

By this action the General Conference Committee provided for the care of every one of the inmates who entered either home of Adventist people, and would not allow the two homes to continue half in the church and half out. No more would they be regarded as church institutions, but would be viewed as appendages to the Sanitarium and the Sanitarium management.

During this turbulent time, the Sanitarium management opened a Rescue Home[61] for women on the old Austin farm which adjoined the Haskell Home property. Louis C. Leake and his wife, Dr. Ruth Bryant Leake, a graduate nurse and registered physician, assumed management of the institution. This was needed as Battle Creek expanded from a large country town to a growing city, with corresponding sociological problems. Young women who found themselves unfortunately situated through an adverse trend of circumstances would have the privilege of home comforts for a nominal fee. This charge was commensurate to their circumstances, or they could chose to assist with the work of the home in payment for the care and medical attention provided. They would also be taught to live better lives, both morally and physically in the hope that a general improvement might result in their lives.

By September, 1907, followers of the Seventh-day Adventist Church, had withdrawn their support from the Haskell Home because it was non-sectarian and because of Dr. Kellogg's ungodliness. What hurt more was S.D.A. members removing their children from the home. As a result, classes had their numbers depleted forcing the management to put the few children remaining out in families. On October 1, the Home was closed until spring. The James White Memorial Home for the aged and the new Rescue Home for women remained open.

---

[61] In the October 25, 1908 edition of the *Sunday Journal-Record*, there was a lengthy article about the first anniversary of the Bethesda Maternity Home on the Austin farm. There were nine babies delivered since the dedication. It remained in operation until February, 1913.

There are no records from the Haskell Home that exist, but based upon various sources, the number of children over the years were:

SOURCE	DATE	INMATES
Newspaper	Apr. 1893	30
The Bible Echo	Jul. 1896	85
Appeal	Oct. 1897	111
Appeal	Apr. 1898	120
Appeal	Oct. 1898	100
Newspaper	Apr. 1903	110
Appeal	Oct. 1903	107[62]
Appeal	Oct. 1904	avg. 100
SOURCE	DATE	INMATES
Newspaper	Jan. 1905	112
Appeal	Apr. 1905	105
Newspaper	Nov. 1905	129
Appeal	Apr. 1906	about 100
Appeal	Aug. 1907	25
Newspaper	Feb. 1909	37
Newspaper	Feb. 1911	50

Even after the Haskell Home was "disinherited" by the Adventist Church in 1907, nine children – six girls and three boys remained. During the winter, they occupied the cottage on the grounds near the main building, thus avoiding much unnecessary expense. An effort was made to make the Haskell Home self-supporting and to this end the 67 acres of good farming land was used. There were also several thousand fruit trees, and during the winter the dairy production was profitable with four cows, earning enough to allow the purchase of seven more. The Home was opened again about June, 1908 to meet the frequent applications for the admission of children.

Although Dr. John H. Kellogg was disfellowshipped by the Church in 1907, he continued all their practices including a vegetarian diet and daily exercise until his death on December 14, 1943, at the age of 91.

---

[62] Primary, 36; Intermediate, 32; Grammar Department, 39.

Chapter 12.

February 4, 1909

Rosa Lee had already had a hard life. Her parents were both killed in an interurban wreck[63] in Illinois when she was a year old. Rosa escaped without a scratch and was found in the wreckage clinging to her Mother's body. Mr. J. T. Holcomb heard the impact from his nearby farm and was the first to render aid to the injured and carried Rosa to his home where she remained for the next two years.

Reverses came to the Holcomb family, which consisted of the parents and seven children. After reading of the Haskell Home in the *Battle Creek Journal*, it was decided to place the girl in that institution. They travelled to Battle Creek, met with Mr. Owen and made all the necessary arrangements to place Rosa in the Home, but by the time the paperwork was completed, it was late in the evening. Rather than transfer a sleeping babe and have her wake in a strange environment, they decided to keep her one more night and drop her off the next morning.

February 5, 1909

Superintendent Owen and his wife were sleeping in a room on the third floor, the same floor as the boys of the Haskell Home.

"I was awakened by my wife, who cried 'There's a fire!' Jumping from my bed, I found the room filled with smoke and

---

[63] Possibly the head-on collision between a train and an express car heavily loaded with freight on the Charleston and Mattoon interurban line at 10:30 o'clock A.M., Friday morning, August 30, 1907. The train was on its way to Charleston to attend the Coles county fair, and the car in which they were riding was crowded to its capacity. Eighteen persons were killed and about sixty passengers were injured. Both cars were going about thirty miles an hour and met as they were rounding a sharp curve. The impact was so terrific that the passenger car was telescoped. The only couple in the fatality list were Sylvanus F. and Martha Enos.

Willard Library Digital Collections
LPC-035-012-001A

LPC-035-016-004A[64]

LPC-035-013-002A

---

[64] Caption: This shows the south side after part of the east side had fallen in.

LPC-035-016-004A

LPC-035-016-002A[65]

LPC-035-013-004A

---

[65] Caption: Alarm turned in at 1:19 A.M. Bldg had been burning about 40 min. before that. This view shows front side and main entrance of bldg at south-east corner. A strong wind was blowing from the south.

LPC-035-012-002A

LPC-035-017-001A[66]

LPC-035-016-003A

---

[66] Caption: A view of the N.W. corner after the walls began to come down. Goguac Lake did not hold enough water to put out this one. [The top of the two solitary vertical windows was the escape for the children who jumped before the floor gave away and one girl disappeared from view.]

the halls to be in even worse condition.   My wife and I awakened the boys and she steered them down the stairs amidst total darkness to safety."

Mrs. Owen continued "I had ten of my little ones with me shortly after we discovered the fire and had turned to leave the building, with the little children hanging on to my dress when I remembered Donald Webber[67], a six-week-old babe. We all started back after him and fought our way through the flames and half-choked and strangling from the smoke, we reached the babe and then carrying it under one arm, with little Edwin Hussey[68], a three-year-old under the other, we started on the return through the burning halls, the entire brood still clinging to me. Thank God, we were able to make our way out again in safety."

Clad only in his trousers, Mr. Owen rushed downstairs to send in a fire alarm. Forced to fight his way through falling timbers, smoke and flames to the telephone, located in a rear room where the fire had gained more headway, he yelled "Fire! Fire in Haskell Home" into the receiver, but the line was dead.

Mary Armstrong, the oldest girl in the school awoke suddenly, discovering the third floor where she was quartered was filled with smoke. Below could be heard the crackling of flames. The female dormitory was in the northwest corner of the building, and the two means of exit were by the back stairs and an outside fire escape. Mary groped her way through the darkness to the back stairway to find escape impossible because of the dense smoke and flames which were licking their way to the top floor. She discovered that the outside fire escape in another part of the building was impossible to reach.

Mary woke the other girls, but when they sprang from their beds, the floor beneath them was so hot that they were unable to stand up in their bare feet. Several climbed onto

---

[67] Died Aug 14, 1909 from cholera infantum at the Haskell Home. Buried in Haskell Home Cemetery.

[68] Son of Mrs. Hussey, an employee of the Stewart Laundry, whose husband was in a Toronto hospital, where he had been transferred from Flint.

chairs. Gathering the smaller girls around her, the older girl felt her way back to the room where everything was burning to a window on the west end of the room and told them the only thing to do was to jump."

Below she saw her brother, James, aged fourteen, who with most boys had been ushered to safety by Superintendent and Mrs. Owen. He was standing on the roof of a coal-shed, two stories below.

Mary did not waver. Seizing two of the smaller girls, one who happened to be her sister, she held them down as far as she could and let them drop into the arms of her sturdy young brother, who caught them as best he could and so broke their falls. Pearl Armstrong, aged 8, and Bernice Edwards, aged 5, were rescued in this way.

But the boy was unable to hold the rest as they fell. Seven of the little ones, clad only in their night-clothes, jumped the entire distance to safety, miraculously escaping injury. Among these were Violet Armstrong, 11; Mable Ruth Cooper, 11; Ruth Ross, 10 and Myrtle May Conners, 8.

"I was awakened by the screams of my sister Mary," said Violet Armstrong, shortly after the fire. "I tried to find my way to the door but the smoke drove me back. Then I went to the window and was knocked senseless when I landed below. My hair and eyebrows were burned by the flames in the room."

The last two girls to stand by the window were Mary Armstrong and Cecil Coutant.

"Jump," cried the older girl.

"I'm afraid," replied Cecil.

Unable to withstand the stifling smoke any longer, Mary jumped and landed on the roof of the coal-shed, twenty-five feet below. Because she struck her head on the ground, her fall stunned her, and she next remembered being carried into the nearby house of Mr. A. Hempstead, the gardener of the institution.

Seventy-five years later, 85-year-old Oren Confer related that he and his late brother, Ivan, were residents of the home when the blaze broke out. "We had been there three years when the fire struck. I can still see James Armstrong waking up the boys. There were a dozen of us in the boys' dormitory. We got out by the stairs and in our nightgowns marched or ran across the snow to the old laundry building in the back. I can still see Miss Armstrong shoving some of the girls out the window of their wing onto the coal shed roof." Oren spent that night at Dr. Kellogg's home. His brother died in 1981 at the age of 80.

The only other inmates of the doomed structure were Mrs. Lillian Scott and her two children who were also occupying a room on the third floor. Mrs. Scott, who was in a delicate condition, was awakened by the screams of the girls in their room, grabbed her children and fought her way through the flames to the ground floor. All were seriously burned, the little boy's hair being singed from his head.

Dr. John H. Kellogg was among the first to arrive on the scene. He promptly assisted in the care of the children, directing some to his spacious home on Manchester Street and the rest to the Hempstead cottage in the rear of the main building.

The alarm was turned in about 1:25 by night operator Briggs, at the Citizen's Telephone Exchange. He heard the call come in, but all he could catch were the words "Fire, Fire, Home" before the line went dead. Realizing the wires were probably disconnected by the effect of the flames, left him wondering what "home" was in danger. With rare presence of mind he rushed to another room where the main telephone indicator was located and ascertained from which line the call had originated. This only narrowed down the region of the city. Using his best judgment, Mr. Briggs assumed the fire was at the Haskell Home and at once notified the central fire station. Within five minutes water was being thrown on the burning building.

Soon after the arrival of the firemen, the roof of the north wing caved in and the walls began to totter. A driving wind drove the flames into the rest of the building and although several streams of water, supplemented by fire engine service were kept playing on the building, all efforts were fruitless. By three o'clock the building was a total loss and all that remained was the tottering walls and the blazing timbers. It was too great a conflagration for the firemen to cope with, while the distance of the home from the nearest fire station practically eliminated the various engine companies from any further usefulness than to prevent a spreading of the flames to other structures. Even the rescue of the children had been effected before either Engine Co. No. 2 or No. 4 reached the scene – the nearest corps of fire fighters. Even with a hose line directed to all five floors, it could not be contained, partly because of the heat. One fire-fighter commented that "it made a person think it was a second edition of Hell and then some." One lone chimney and a few charred corners alone remained of the large three-story brick structure. Even the shed which aided the seven girls in escaping from the third floor was entirely consumed.

Somewhat isolated from the city itself, the Haskell Home burned to the cellar before the greater part of Battle Creek knew that there had been an outbreak of fire.

Of the 31 children in the home that night, three lost their young lives in the fire:

Lena McKelvey was the baby of the family, aged 14. Her Mother placed her in the institution only recently, taking occasional treatments at the Sanitarium. She was being treated for an injured hand while her family visited Florida, where they expected to remain a month. She saw her brothers frequently during that time and seemed pleased with her surroundings. On the Sunday before the fire, she spent with her brothers at their Champion Street home. She was survived by her Mother, five brothers and a sister, namely Hugh E., 31; Newell A., 29; Allen, 26; Victor E., 23 of Battle Creek; and Audley A., 17 of Climax. The sister was Mrs. Grace E. Hawkins, 33. Superintendent Owen stated that she was an extremely quiet child, and may not have awakened by the noise attending the discovery of the fire. The other girls did not remember having seen her in the confusion which marked their escape from the burning structure. Several days later, her brother, who resided with relatives in Battle Creek, wended his way through the mass of hot brick, twisted irons, heat and smoke, in the vain endeavor to locate the remains of his sister.

Lena McKelvey and her Mother, Mrs. J. P. Clegg.
Newspaper photo.

Cecil Coutant, age 12, had been in the home for seven years, coming from Iowa. She refused to jump with Mary Armstrong and witnesses saw her standing at the window. While watching her companions jump, she took a step back from the window. A loud crash was heard and the next minute the Coutant girl disappeared from sight. She had a sister living with Dr. Rowland Harris of the Sanitarium and her brother was spending the winter in the home of a farmer near Urbandale.

George Goodnow, age 10, came from Chattanooga, Tennessee, a year before. According to Superintendent Owen "The little fellow was one of those unfortunates who didn't know how old he was. We called him ten years of age. He had a habit of wrapping himself up – head and all – in his blankets at night, and had to be repeatedly cautioned against this. When the fire occurred he was probably caught in this way. He could have dropped out of his window a distance of twelve or fifteen feet to safety on the roof of the balcony below, but apparently he never attempted escape this way.[69]"

Fireman Albert J. (Jack) Burrows[70], of No. 4 station, was badly cut on the wrist by a piece of falling glass which required seven stitches in his arm. There were a number of narrow escapes – several times firemen were nearly cut off from escape by the fire traveling so rapidly through the building. On one occasion three firemen who were working well up in the corner of the building stepped into a basement door for a minute, and a second later a huge section of brick wall landed just where they had stood, covering the hose.

Ruth Ross, one of the girls who jumped from the building sustained serious injuries in her back.[71]

There were thirty-seven children in the building on the night of the fire, and except for the seven who jumped, all left by the stairs, as all four fire escapes were cut off by the fire.

The next morning a group of little ones were gathered around, partly clad in whatever could be found for them, or still in their night-clothes. Several nurses from the Sanitarium were on hand to minister to the orphans, many of whom sustained minor injuries, burns and bruises.

Several children agreed that when they sprang from their beds the floor beneath them was so hot that they were unable to

---

[69] George Goodnow was one of the Negroes brought to the Haskell Home by Mrs. Steele. He was normally quartered in the boys dormitory, but on the morning of the fire, he was nowhere to be seen.

[70] Albert J. Burrows, son of William Henry Borrows and Viola Eudora Angella Huggett, born April 25, 1874 in Pennfield, Michigan. Married March 21, 1906, Clara Louise Bottomly in Battle Creek. Died July 26, 1950 in Battle Creek. Buried at Hicks cemetery, Pennfield, Michigan.

[71] There was no following story regarding her injuries, so they may not have been as severe as first thought.

stand up in their bare feet. In fact several climbed onto chairs. Just before they jumped to safety they felt the floor giving under them. Just after Mary leaped to the shed roof, two stories below, a crash above was heard and it was believed that the floor gave way beneath the Coutant girl, precipitating her plunge into the fiery depths below.

Mary Armstrong, the young heroine, sat rocking a six-weeks-old babe and told her story in a quiet, unassuming manner. Her head was bound in a large bandage because of the bruises she had sustained in her long jump to safety.[72] She was one of thirteen children whose home was in Iowa. Five of them were in the home at the time of the fire and the one boy was spending the winter on a farm in Bedford. Mary had

been at the Home the previous four years and attending sixth grade at No. 3 school. She was sent to the Sanitarium for rest and treatment.

Several of the children were taken by a couple of Sanitarium nurses, three boys were placed in the home of William Robinson, Miss Lena Steinel took two children, Cassius Messenger aged one, and Frank Ripley, aged five.

---

[72] Newspaper photo.

Several others were still at the residence of Dr. Kellogg, while Superintendent and Mrs. Owen, Mrs. Lillian Scott and several children were still at the home of George Hempstead.

Mrs. Lillian Sprague, who had but recently placed her three boys in the home, was overjoyed at the sight of her little ones safe and sound. The services of a nurse were required to quiet her.

Several days passed until the debris could be safely inspected for the remains of the missing children or the cause of the fire. Several fireman participated in the search and four to five feet of ashes were shifted through the basement floor. Scattered through this were tons of brick, mortar, scrap iron, and other debris. Nothing resembling human bones were found until February 8. A charred portion of a bone, supposedly a part of the arm of George Goodnow, the colored boy, seemed to be the humerus, or upper part of the arm together with the joint, about four inches in length. Blackened and charred, it was a ghastly relic among the debris thrown into the basement, underneath the room which he occupied at the time of the fire. The site was a Mecca of curiosity seekers and several persons discovered poking around the ruins were ordered to desist.

Chief Weeks[73] believed that the fire originated from the dust chute, being caused by spontaneous combustion. The chute, used for the sweepings of floor dust and dirt extended from the third floor down to the basement. He believed that this accumulation of debris caught fire spontaneously, the draft carrying the flames to the second and third stories, where it

---

[73] Known as W. P. Weeks, few knew his full name of Washington Plato Weeks. His half-brother, Joseph, was a lieutenant in the twentieth Michigan Infantry and concluded his Civil War service before W. P. was born on May 17, 1865. He started as a volunteer fireman at the age of 15, when hose carts were pulled by hand. He had a dominant role in the transition which replaced prancing horses with modern motorized vehicles. He was the oldest firefighter in the United States when he retired after 61 years of firefighting, serving 49 consecutive years as fire chief. He died July 6, 1952.

burst out simultaneously. This would account for the fire gaining such a headway in the north wing of the building, the dust chute being located in this part of the structure, coming up through the third floor, close to the room where the girls were quartered.

By February 9th the careful and systematic work of searching for some traces of the remains of the children strengthened the belief that the small bodies were completely incinerated in the fiery furnace. However several men continued the work, in spite of the rain and snow. Finally, the discovery of a mass of charred flesh, evidently from the shoulder and including a portion of the spinal column was found, undoubtedly all that remained of the little McKelvey girl. This conclusion was reached from the fact that the flesh was wrapped in a blackened mass of cloth, evidently a bed quilt or blanket. As Cecil Coutant had reached the windows, but did not dare to jump, and as Lena McKelvey had apparently not been awakened at all, there seems little question but that these remnants of a human frame belonged to the Battle Creek girl.

Also found was a jaw-bone containing several teeth. The authorities believed that they were from the skull of Lena McKelvey. Nearby were found one or two small bones, one evidently a finger, which were put into a package, to be turned over to the police.

The find was made in the northwest part of the building but somewhat remote from the spot that had been marked as the probable place for finding the bodies. Probably the bodies slid to the nearer corner of the room when the floor fell in to the basement.

Superintendent Owen found a clock while groping his way to the basement to find some shoes, as he had escaped in his bare feet. The clock was stopped at 1:25, which fixed the time of the blaze.

In spite of the main building destruction, two little boys arrived from Benton Harbor February 9, and joined the greater part of the children being cared for in the building that had not burned, which was used for laundry. Fifteen sleeping rooms were repapered and kalsomined for the temporary use of the children. The building had hot and cold water, was heated by steam and had all the necessary sanitary arrangements, making it very comfortable.

Through the ruins of the building wandered a little lad, with tear bedimmed eyes. When the *Journal* reporter asked him what he was looking for, he looked up pathetically and replied, "I'm looking for my Christmas presents, sir. They were in my room and I thought maybe I could find them if there was anything left of them." The little fellow trudged on with tears running down his cheeks.

Steven Chovin, now four, the lad who recently arrived from north-eastern Michigan, awoke Friday morning in the Hempstead cottage crying for the one possession from his past. "Where's my satchel?"

Mary Armstrong, the oldest girl in the school saved seven lives that night. She was extremely reluctant to talk much of her heroism, but told the following story: "I woke up about one o'clock, I guess, and looked through the windows. I then woke up the rest of the girls who slept in the room with me. They were all younger than I. I went to see if we could get down the fire escapes, but we couldn't, so I took the girls back to the room where everything was burning and told them the only thing to do was to jump, I took the smallest ones and held them down as far as I could and then let them drop. My brother was below and tried to catch them I think. I waited as long as I could and then I jumped myself." The story was told by the girl with the tears running from her eyes while a Sanitarium nurse dressed the burns on her head and other injuries received through the drop from the third floor.

James Armstrong, the boyish hero also talked modestly of his share in the girls' escape. "I knew the only thing for the girls to do was to jump," he said, "so I tried to get them to. Of course they were scared like the rest of us, but they did the best they could."

A benefit evening of entertainment for the Haskell Home

sufferers was given at the Sanitarium chapel on February 10. Like so many visits before the children filed in, two by two, but this time there were three broken gaps where the missing children would have been in the usual formation. The Sanitarium orchestra played while Miss Bonnie Core gave a violin solo and William Drever a trombone solo. Dr. John H. Kellogg gave a history of the Home, illustrated by stereopticon views, and some of the children, together with Mr. and Mrs. Owen described their experiences during the fire.

Although she had the courage and presence of mind to force seven children to jump from the third story window, Mary Armstrong was too modest to appear before the audience at the Sanitarium.

In response to the question of why couldn't all the children be saved by going down the steps with Mrs. Owen, Mr. Owen explained:

"Haskell Home, which formerly fronted on Hubbard Street, was composed of three 'L's which ran back from the street, or another description was that the building was shaped like the letter 'E'. On the north side and in the back west room slept the nine girls. Around in the middle 'L' and separated from this room by a corridor, stairs leading to the second story and a long hall was the room which Mrs. Owen and myself, together with the smaller children occupied. When the fire broke out and Mrs. Owen and I woke up we could look out of our west window and see the flames in the room which the girls occupied. I thought of the smaller children first and turned my attention to them. Mrs. Owen and and I led them in the darkness through a long hall to the south 'L' where stairs led down to the second story and then to the first floor. When we had gotten the smaller children out I went back to the building and made an effort to reach the room where the girls were located. But the fire, which evidently originated in the back stairs in the south 'L' cutting off escape by these stairs for the girls, also cut me off from reaching them. The girls could not get to the stairs we had gone down for the reason that the fierce flames and smoke prevented exit past the burning back stairs near their room. So the girls, cut off from escape by either the front or back, were caught in the fire trap."

Dr. Kellogg wrote a letter to the editor of the *Battle Creek Journal* that appeared on the front page of the February 10, 1909 edition. He thanked the banks, merchants, several ladies' societies and scores of friends who made generous contributions of money, clothing, shoes and other necessities. He also clarified the confusion of the ownership that had been in the press of late, regarding the Seventh Day Adventist church. He recounted how the gift of Mrs. Haskell made the Home possible, and her condition that the Home should be non-sectarian and undenominational, and his assurance that the charter of the institution stipulated this when incorporated. The money raised by the Seventh-day Adventist denomination was used in purchasing, equipping and carrying on the James White Memorial Home, which had been a refuge for the old people of the S.D.A. denomination. Semi-annual collections within the faith provided for operating the Haskell Home but that had been completely cut off for years. He also pledged to rebuild on the cottage plan and made practically fireproof to avoid risk of possible loss of life in the future.

The *Battle Creek Enquirer* printed a rebuttal by Elder A. G. Daniels contesting the implication that the S.D.A. was responsible for the founding based on the resolutions passed by the Seventh-day Adventist General Conference, March 22, 1891. Mrs. Haskell was a generous donor and should receive due credit for her gift, but the founding and entire work was carried on by the denomination, and the larger share of money used in the enterprise was supplied by the S.D.A. The property was conveyed by deeds to the S.D.A. Medical Missionary and Benevolent Association. In the latter part of 1898 either the Trustees, or the officers of this Medial Missionary and Benevolent Association formed a separate Corporation for both the Haskell Home and the James White Memorial Home. The records state that the reason for doing this was to place each institution on a basis which would enable either to receive legacies, but it was expressly stated in the minutes that the deeds should still be held by the Medical Missionary and Benevolent Association. This arrangement continued until April 18, 1904, when the Trustees of the Medical Missionary and Benevolent Association "authorized, empowered and directed" the President and Secretary of the Association to deliver both deeds for these respective properties. This was done without the approval of the constituency which the Trustees represented, or the knowledge of the denomination who had established and maintained these institutions from their inception.

This was followed by clarifications and additional allegations by Dr. Kellogg, Elders, and readers.

There was no investigation of the Haskell Home holocaust, despite the fact that three lives were lost. Coroner H. H. Bidwell could see no necessity for holding an inquest, since no demand had been made by an official delving into the cause of the fire. The few human remains found in the ruins were the result of a fire – a fact quite beyond dispute.

Chapter 13.

It didn't take long for the rumors to spread. On the morning of the fire, the front page of the newspaper reviewed a list of fires that were Adventist properties:

DATE	PLACE	LOSS	CAUSE
June 1, 1891	Sanitarium Engine Room	$22,000	gasoline expl.
Jan. 11, 1893	Battle Creek College Bldg	7,000	unknown
Feb. 3, 1896	Sanitarium Health Food Co.	12,000	unknown
July 19, 1898	Sanitarium Health Food Co.	10,500	incendiary
April 12, 1900	Sanitary Nut Food Co.	5,200	explosion
July 21, 1900	Old Food Factory	10,500	unknown
April 27, 1901	College Building	5,300	unknown
Feb. 18, 1902	Sanitarium and Hospital	250,000	unknown
Dec. 30, 1902	Review and Herald	300,000	unknown
May 18, 1903	Sanitarium Barn	4,000	incendiary
July 10, 1905	Sanitarium Ice House	1,800	unknown
Feb. 5, 1909	Haskell Home	50,000	unknown

This should be put in perspective, as there were 103 fires that destroyed Battle Creek buildings in 1909. Most building in the city were wooden structures, heated and lighted by burning wood, coal, gas, kerosene, or other flammable products. This was typical for the time which was why there were many fires in every town across the nation. Fire investigation wasn't the science it is today, which accounts for the many unknown designations above. Even with all these losses to property, it was remarkable that only one life was lost in the 1902 Sanitarium fire and just three lives lost in the 1909 Haskell Home fire.

It was known that the fire started in the northwest portion of the building, yet Superintendent Owen declared that there was no heat source of any sort in that part of the building. The building was heated by steam and the steam pipes ran in from an adjacent building, which eliminated the heating of the building as a possible cause. The theory that the fire might have started from defective electric wiring was dropped when it was learned that there was no electric wiring in the building, except for the telephone wires.[74]

"From all appearances the fire started in the basement", stated Chief Weeks, "because it was there that it gained its greatest headway. When we arrived on the scene the entire north wing was in flames."

The ruins of the burned structure told the awful story of the veneer building made up of a wooden frame covered with a single brick wall. The absence of cross walls gave the fire full sway to sweep its destruction in its path. There was also a total absence of fire walls in the building that might have hindered the progress of the inferno.

Georgia pine was used throughout in the construction of the building. Dry and full of pitch, it made a fierce blaze and gave off an intense heat. Days later a round ball which looked as though it might be a human head was unearthed. Acting Mayor Nichols gingerly picked it out of the ashes. But a careful examination showed that the ball was just a bundle of carpet rags, bound so tightly they refused to burn. When they were thrown out and came in contact with fresh air, they burst into flames, so intense was the heat.

Like all other Sanitarium buildings, there was a complete and elaborate system of ventilation. There were several large air ducts leading from the basement to the attic. These were built of wood, and when a spark dropped into one of these it was changed into a roaring flue. Several times, firemen working in the attic were nearly cut off by the flames working their way in back of them through these air ducts. These ducts assisted in the spread of the flames and one of them running through the building at the end of the hall to the North wing, evidently cut the girls off from making their escape through the building. The building was partly equipped with fire escapes but there were none on the extreme end of the north wing where the girls were quartered, and the children were unable to

---

[74] Originally the Haskell Home had its own lighting plant, but this burned in the Laundry building fire of 1903 and the dynamo was never replaced. Since that laundry fire, oil lamps were used for illumination.

reach any of the rooms that had access to an outside escape.

The heroism of Mary Anderson and her younger brother, James, did not go unnoticed. Their thoughtfulness of others in their hour of peril was remarkable. Her courage was brought before the Carnegie Hero Fund Commission and she was expected to receive this recognition according to the front page of the March 10, 1909 *Battle Creek Daily Moon*.[75]

The day after the fire, hundreds of postal card views of the Haskell Home ruins and of the building before the fire, were sold by the dealers in this city. Police roped off the grounds in an effort to keep sightseers and camera fiends away from the wreckage.

There was much initial speculation of how the fire started, but M. W. Wentworth, steward of the Sanitarium agreed with Fire chief Weeks that it started in the dust chute. Dust is very liable to spontaneous combustion, and in the Haskell Home there was a wooden chute from the attic to the basement, with openings for each floor. When the rooms were swept, the dust was dumped down this chute, which was cleaned out from time to time, from an opening for this purpose in the basement. Along with dust, the thread and bits of material from the sewing rooms would have been added to the mix. No one could remember the last time this accumulation of dust and debris was emptied. Since this chute was situated in the end of the north wing of the building where the fire was first discovered, it seemed the likely cause. The draft carrying the flames to the second and third stories, where it burst out simultaneously would account for the fire gaining such headway in the north wing of the building where the girls were quartered.

The total insurance on the Haskell Home amounted to $29,875, of which $26,750 was in the building itself and $3,125 on the contents. The policies were spread over sixteen companies ranging from $1,000 to $2,000 each. The replacement value of the Home had risen to $50,000[76]. Dr.

---

[75] She was not one of the 132 awarded for acts performed in 1909.

[76] $1.4 million adjusted for inflation.

Kellogg vowed to rebuild the Haskell Home, but on a cottage plan, where each family would have their own little home with shared classrooms and dining facilities.   The immediate solution for the Haskell Home that once provided a home for over one hundred orphans, was moved into the much smaller laundry building that could only accommodate about forty children.   It operated on this reduced scale for a few more years.

The large orchard and garden made the institution almost self-supporting.   The boys occupied their spare time in preparing strawberry boxes for the coming crop. The Home, in the former power plant and laundry presented a very flourishing appearance, and those quarters were, in many ways, more convenient for work than the larger home.

The Feb. 5, 1909 *Battle Creek Daily Moon* printed on page one, all the children that were in the Home at the time of the fire, including Cecil Coutant and George Goodnow as missing, but listed Lena McClevy along with the other survivors:

In July, 1910, an article appeared in the *Daily Moon* that the board, of which Dr. J. H. Kellogg was a member, decided to plat the Haskell Home grounds into building lots and the children moved into the country on a farm.

In June of 1912, thirty acres of the old property was sold, bounded on the east by

* * * * * * * * * * * * *

THOSE WHO WERE SAVED.
The following thirty-one children were in the Home at the time of the fire:

Frances Owen,
Mertie May Conner,
Kirk Sprague,
Jesse Sprague,
Carl Sprague,
Harold Owen,
Ivan Confer,
Orin Confer,
Mabel Ruth Confer,
Ruth Ross,
Mary Armstrong,
James Armstrong,
Violet Armstrong,
Helen Izora Armstrong,
Pearl Armstrong,
Cecil Coutant (missing)
Ruth Moyer,
Charles Ross Moyer,
Myrtle Dacon,
Ephrosene Esther Herrick,
Howard Waller,
Lloyd Scott,
George Goodenow (missing),
Lena McClevy,
Steven Chovin,
Edwin Hussey,
Donald Webber,
Sylina Scott,
Bernice Edwards,
George Lathrop.

* * * * * * * * * * * * *

Hubbard Street, on the west by Jordan Street, on the south by Graves Street and on the north by Haskell Street, netting $30,000. There were 75 lots, which sold for $300 to $350 each, with instructions to I. W. Schram, real estate dealer, to let Sanitarium helpers and guests have first choice. The remaining property was platted to be sold, with the plan to find a suitable location several mile west of the Sanitarium to build another structure. This new building, including the grounds was estimated to cost $100,000.

An article in the Battle Creek *Moon Journal* on January 2, 1926, announced that the Haskell Home property was transferred to Battle Creek College, having been closed for about a year. The deed was filed with Frank Eddy, Register of Deeds, in the court house at Marshall, Michigan. Among new uses for this property were new dormitories, a field house and football field, and a nursery with experimental purposes in growing material that would ultimately be transferred to the arboretum. Work on razing the power house and laundry building occurred in April, 1933, with the materials salvaged from the structure given to the unemployed men doing the work. When cleared, this was the site of the new Battle Creek College athletic field.

In 1943, The National Housing Administration constructed one hundred temporary houses between Hubbard and Welch Streets, to relieve the housing shortage. Mayor Bernard E. Goode suggested the name of "Haskell Homes" for the project, reviving the memory of the former orphanage that was once located in that vicinity.

In 1949, construction crews digging cellars for residential homes on Bernardo Place, located halfway between Hubbard and Jordan Streets, discovered the foundation and some of the charred wooden remains of the original Haskell Home.

The eerie headline of the November 30, 1952 Battle Creek *Enquirer and News* was "TWO CHILDREN DIE IN SEPARATE FIRES HERE TWO OTHERS HURT AT HASKELL HOME." The home was a six-apartment building in the Haskell Homes housing project on Welch Avenue.

Frank Smith was seriously burned on the hands and ankles while cleaning out a paint brush near the water heater. The fumes from the paint thinner were presumably exploded by the flame of the water heater. A daughter, Sonja, 5, ran from the house when the blast set fire to her hair and pajamas, and after racing half way around the building in panic, she was stopped and rolled in the snow by a neighbor, Ray Waldo, who occupied the apartment next to the Smiths. Mrs. Smith seized another daughter, Penny, 3, and ran to a neighbor's apartment. Their eight-year-old daughter, Tonnie Kay was found in front of an easy chair in the living room, where she had been sitting when the blast sent flames across the apartment.

Both Mr. and Mrs. Smith were treated at Leila hospital for their burns and admitted, along with Sonja, who suffered burns on her forehead, scalp, chest, shoulders and back.

Four other families were in the building and ran outside when they felt the blast and saw smoke and soot puff in from the ceiling and walls.

Sergeant Clyde Craft of Percy Jones Army hospital sent his wife and two daughters to safety outside and then soaked a quilt in water and ran to the Smith apartment, hoping to rescue Tonnie, but by then the interior was a mass of flames. Sgt. Craft stopped several other men from trying to enter the holocaust to save the girl. "No one could have lived in there," he said afterward.

Tonnie Kay had been deaf, probably since birth, and it was to give this child the extra advantages of training and instruction at the Ann J. Kellogg School that the family had moved here from Cadillac, Michigan in December, 1949. She began mastering some words and the family had rising hopes that she could correct her hearing handicap.

The WWII defense housing named Haskell Homes was leveled about 1965, thus ending another era of the Haskell Home orphanage site.

Haskell Home, Battle Creek, MI
1900 Population Census

NAME	REL	C	S	DOB		AE	POB	OCC[77]
Lang, Ocie M.	Roomer	W	F	Sep	1877	22	PA	Mother
Hanly, Harry	Member	W	M	Apr	1891	9	NJ	School
Arnold, Curtis	Member	W	M	Apr	1889	11	IN	School
Meacham, Maggie E.	Head	W	F	Nov	1877	22	PA	Mothr
Hunter, James	Member	B	M	Feb	1891	9	AL	School
Chester, Ezra	Member	B	M	May	1892	8	MO	School
Turner, Willis	Member	B	M	Nov	1892	9	AL	School
Rounds, Roy	Member	W	M	Mar	1891	9	MI	School
White, Oscar	Member	W	M	Dec	1891	9	MI	School
McFarrens, Henry	Member	W	M	Jan	1892	8	OH	School
Libert, Raymond	Member	W	M	Jul	1892	7	OH	School
Carion, William	Member	W	M	Unk	1893	6	MI	School
Stockford, Max	Member	W	M	Aug	1891	8	MI	School
Delaney, Jennie	Member	W	F	Mar	1893	7	MI	School
Huntley, Clayton	Member	W	M	May	1892	8	VT	School
Park, Ada A.	Head	W	F	Jul	1867	32	MO	Mother
Park, Edith W	Member	W	F	Sep	1892	7	MO	School
Park, Orl R.	Member	W	M	Jan	1898	2	MO	
Park, Hallie	Member	W	F	Jan	1899	4/12	MO	
Park, Roy F.	Member	W	M	Nov	1885	14	MO	School
Randall, Louie	Member	W	F	Sep	1883	16	OH	School
Comins, John S.	Head	W	M	Dec	1844	55	MA	Super
Comins, Celestia	Wife	W	F	Mar	1849	51	MA	Matron
Owens, Christeen	Member	W	F	Dec	1881	18	IA	Helper
White, Eva	Member	W	F	Nov	1886	14	MI	Helper
Taylor, Walter	Member	W	M	Jan	1894	5	IL	School
Brown, Paul	Member	W	M	Mar	1897	3	MI	
Brown, Floyd	Member	W	M	Jun	1899	11/12	MI	
Brown, Ferne	Member	W	F	Jun	1899	11/12	MI	
Curran, Howard	Member	W	M	May	1897	3	MI	
Park, Fay	Member	W	M	Jan	1891	9	MO	School
Park, Guy	Member	W	M	Jul	1888	11	KS	School
Corkham, George V.	Member	W	M	Feb	1884	16	NoSc	School
Denison, Robert	Member	W	M	Dec	1884	15	MI	School
Odell, Oden	Member	W	B	Oct	1885	14	AL	School
DeHaven, Walter A.	Member	W	M	Jul	1886	13	VA	School

[77] Column headers used: Name, Relation to Head of Household, Color, Sex, Month & Year of Birth, Place of Birth and Occupation.

Haskell Home, Battle Creek, MI
1900 Population Census

NAME	REL	C	S	DOB		AE	POB	OCC[78]
Corkham, Cecil	Member	W	M	Oct	1885	14	NoSc	School
Banden, Wesley	Member	W	M	Jul	1885	14	NY	School
Gillis, George	Member	W	M	Nov	1887	12	IL	School
Thompson, Nellie H.	Member	W	F	Jun	1888	11	WI	School
Gillis, William	Member	W	M	Nov	1897	12	IL	School
Foster, Frank	Member	W	M	Apr	1887	13	MI	School
Catella, Pedro	Member	B	M	Nov	1887	12	PoRi	School
Elston, Clay	Member	B	M	Aug	1889	10	AL	School
Lane, Charles F.	Head	W	M	Nov	1871	28	OH	Caretaker
Feakin, Emma W.	Head	W	F	Jul	1859	40	IL	Mother
Hatch, Fred	Member	W	M	Nov	1886	13	CO	School
Hanley, Roy	Member	W	M	Sep	1887	12	MI	School
Pieri, Frank	Member	W	M	Nov	1887	12	MO	School
Symonds, Joseph	Member	W	M	Nov	1887	12	OH	School
Fickel, Albert	Member	W	M	Feb	1888	12	WA	School
Shumway, George	Member	W	M	May	1888	12	NY	School
Walker, Morgan	Member	W	M	Sep	1888	11	MI	School
Partain, Artell	Member	W	M	Nov	1888	11	TX	School
Gruber, Fred	Member	W	M	Sep	1889	10	TX	School
Paine, Sidney	Member	W	M	Jul	1891	8	MI	School
Hunter, Samuel	Member	W	M	Jan	1888	11	AL	School
Maxson, Justena	Head	W	F	Aug	1876	23	NE	Mother
Stockford, Virgil E.	Member	W	M	Nov	1889	10	MI	School
Judd, Earl	Member	W	M	Sep	1890	9	MI	School
Clough, Oral	Member	W	M	Jun	1890	9	MI	School
Shepperd, Theo C.	Member	W	M	Mar	1890	10	IN	School
Miller, Robert	Member	W	M	Jan	1891	9	KS	School
Riley, Delaney	Member	W	M	Jul	1891	8	MI	School
George, Potts	Member	W	M	Aug	1889	10	IN	School
Chester, Clarence	Member	W	M	Feb	1889	11	TN	School
Davis, Ellwood	Member	W	M	Mar	1889	11	OH	School
Walker, Arthur	Member	W	M	Mar	1890	10	MI	School
Cook, Amelia	Head	W	F	Jul	1868	31	PA	Mother
Bjork, Victor	Member	W	M	Mar		10	NY	School
Garcia, Gonzalo A.	Member	W	M	Feb	1889	11	MEX	School
Sheppard, James L.	Member	W	M	Oct	1891	8	Unk	

---

[78] Column headers used: Name, Relation to Head of Household,
Color, Sex, Month & Year of Birth, Place of Birth and
Occupation.

Haskell Home, Battle Creek, MI
1900 Population Census

NAME	REL	C	S	DOB		AE	POB	OCC[79]
Hasteller, Willie A.	Member	W	M	Feb	1892	8	KS	School
Bunn, Glenn	Member	W	M	Jun	1892	7	MI	School
Fanner, Leo	Member	W	M	Mar	1893	7	OH	School
Grove, Amanda	Roomer	W	F	May	1854	45	IN	Housekpr
Swartz, Harry A.	Roomer	W	M	Sep	1871	28		Cook
Hansen, Charles	Member	W	M	Dec	1902	7		School
Prothero, Arthur	Member	W	M	Mar	1892	8	NY	School
Smith, Albert	Member	W	M	Oct	1892	7	CT	School
Simmons, Arthur	Member	W	M	Mar	1893	7	OH	School
Potts, John	Member	W	M	Mar	1894	6	IN	School
McFarren, Calista	Member	W	F	Jan	1886	13	OH	School
Brown, Kate L.	Roomer	W	F	Mar	1853	47	IL	Missiony
Brown, Winefred B.	Roomer	W	F	Jul	1892	7	IND	
Brown, Lawrance W.	Roomer	W	M	Feb	1895	5	TN	
Gordon, Leroy V.	Member	W	M	Jul	1891	8	MI	
Lauls, Lisle	Member	W	F	Mar	1893	7	FL	
Symonds, Myrtle	Member	W	F	Apr	1886	14	OH	School
Bean, Sarah E	Head	W	F	Sep	1858	41	WV	Mother
Seebee, Stella	Member	W	F	Jul	1886	13	NY	School
Maddison, Julia	Member	W	F	Mar	1889	11	AL	School
Rijio, Paulina	Member	ITL	F	Apr	1891	9	OH	School
Cooper, Belle	Member	B	F	Mar	1892	8	VA	School
Madison, Ella	Member	B	F	Mar	1892	8	AL	School
Madison, Mary	Member	B	F	Apr	1894	6	AL	
Rejio, Carlina	Member	ITL	F	Jun	1892	7	OH	School
Symonds, Kittie	Member	W	F	Aug	1895	4	OH	
Rigio, Fernando	Member	ITL	M	May	1896	4	OH	
Muller, Martin	Member	W	M	Jan	1898	2	IL	
Lay, Ineg A.	Head	W	F	May	1857	42	MI	Mother
Chester, Mary	Member	B	F	Jun	1887	13	TN	School
Rigio, Carnilla A.	Member	ITA	F	Oct	1889	10	OH	School
Cooper, Agnes	Member	W	F	Mar	1888	11	IA	School
Fickel, Ethel L.	Member	W	F	Mar	1889	11	Unk	School
White, L. May	Member	W	F	May	1889	11	MI	School
Fonner, Zanna L.	Member	W	F	Jun	1890	9	WV	School
Nelson, Anna B.	Member	B	F	Mar	1890	10	TN	School

---

[79] Column headers used: Name, Relation to Head of Household,
Color, Sex, Month & Year of Birth, Place of Birth and
Occupation.

Haskell Home, Battle Creek, MI
1900 Population Census

NAME	REL	C	S	DOB		AE	POB	OCC[80]
Oden, Mamie	Member	B	F	Dec	1890	9	AL	School
Gestner, Alta	Member	W	F	Jun	1887	12	MI	School
Symonds, Lottie	Member	W	F	Mar	1891	9	OH	School
Jaeger, Lillie M.	Head	W	F	Nov	1876	23	IA	Mother
Hostetler, Edith	Member	W	F	Oct	1888	11	KS	School
Fickel, Eva	Member	W	F	Jul	1890	9	OR	School
Garcia, Isabel	Member	I	F	Nov	1890	9	MEX	School
Bjork, Anna	Member	W	F	Apr	1892	8	NY	School
Maxson, Alice	Member	W	F	Jun	1892	7	IA	School
Prothero, C. Ella	Member	W	F	Mar	1894	6	MI	School
Morton, Ida	Member	W	F	Mar	1892	8	IA	School
Seibert, Tanny	Member	W	F	Apr	1894	6	IN	School
Markel, Hasel	Member	W	F	Mar	1894	6	PA	School
A'Delberg, Rosana	Member	W	F	May	1892	8	MI	School
Partain, Bessie	Member	W	F	Apr	1892	8	TX	School
Dawson, Lena M.	Member	W	F	Nov	1891	8	MA	School
Dunn, Nettie A.	Teacher	W	F	Feb	1876	24	IN	Teacher
Tallman, Mary E.	Teacher	W	F	Aug	1880	19	WI	Teacher
Osborn, Ella M.	Teacher	W	F	Apr	1870	30	NY	Teacher
Gormoe, Adolph	Roomer	W	M	May	1832	68	CAN	Grdnr
Readie, Zerada	Head	W	F	Aug	1845	54	OH	Mother
Currme, Howard	Member	W	F	Apr	1897	3	MI	
Currme, William	Member	W	F	Mar	1894	6	MI	
Meacham, Alvina	Housekpr	W	F	Oct	1840	59	PA	Housekpr
Stone, Lizzie	Worker	W	F	Sep	1857	42	MA	Housekpr
Dibble, Tottie	Roomer	W	F	Sep	1877	22	MO	Seamstrs
Mitchell, Bertha M.	Roomer	W	F	Dec	1876	23	OH	Teacher
Thompson, Ella	Roomer	W	F	Nov	1880	19	TN	Teacher
Dehn, Earnestine	Roomer	W	F	Nov	1880	19	LA	Teacher
Lackhorn, Jane	Roomer	W	F	Jun	1874	25	CT	Teacher
Gruel, Minnie	Roomer	W	F	Apr	1882	18	MN	Teacher

---

[80] Column headers used: Name, Relation to Head of Household, Color, Sex, Month & Year of Birth, Place of Birth and Occupation.

Haskell Home, Battle Creek City, MI
Persons who survived the fire are listed in bold print.[81]

NAME	SEX	AGE	P	F	M
Owen, Rodney S.	M	59	MI	NY	MA
Sarah A.	F	53	VT	CAN	VT
Armstrong, Mary E.	F	16	IA	IRE	IRE
James	M	15	IA	IRE	IRE
Herbert	M	14	IA	IRE	IRE
Violet	F	12	IA	IRE	IRE
Helen I.	F	11	IA	IRE	IRE
Pearl	F	9	IA	IRE	IRE
Hill, Francis E.	F	10	IN	US	US
Harold K.	M	8	IN	US	US
Cooper, Mable R.	F	12	OH	unk	unk
Ross, Ruth	F	11	IL	unk	unk
Dacon, Myrtle	F	13	MI	US	US
Masten, Lulu R.	F	9	MI	MI	MI
Charlie R.	F	8	MI	MI	MI
Sprague, Kirk	M	11	MI	OH	OH
Jesse	M	9	MI	OH	OH
Carl	M	8	MI	OH	OH
Scott, Lillian	F	32	WI	GER	NY
Lloyd	M	8	WI	WI	WI
Sylvia	F	6	WI	WI	WI
Wilmer	M	11/12	MI	WI	WI
Ingels, Dixon	M	9	NE	unk	US
Hackney, Charles L.	M	7	MI	MI	GER
Jenna M.	F	5	MI	MI	GER
Stephony, Cecil	M	11	WI	WI	WI
Melvin	M	6	WI	WI	WI
Haver, Cady	M	12	NY	unk	NY
Allen, Willie	M	7	MI	unk	MI
Juckett, Abbie	F	11/12	MI	MI	MI
Watson, Chester A.	M	11	OH	OH	MI
De Witt, Earl	M	5	MI	unk	unk
Pearl	F	5	MI	unk	unk
Edwards, Bernace	F	6	MI	MI	MI
Herrick, Ester E.	F	10	unk	unk	unk
Hutson, Floyd W.	M	4	unk	unk	unk
Confer, Ivan	M	11	MI	MI	MI
Orin	M	9	MI	MI	MI

[81] Column headers used: Name, Sex, Year of Birth, Place of Birth, Father's POB and Mother's POB.

Haskell Home, Battle Creek City, MI[82]

NAME	REL	SEX	AGE	P	F	M
Tappan, Flora	Head	F	59	MN	OH	OH
Frank	Husband	M	60	MN	USA	USA
Jeffrey, Mary	Domestic	F	64	OH	OH	OH
Hackney, Jennie	Inmate	F	14	MI	US	US
Lester, George	Inmate	M	12	MI	US	US
Tiffan, Elmer	Inmate	M	12	MI	MI	MI
Billings, Manley	Inmate	M	9	MI	MI	MI
Hodge, Kenneth	Boarder	M	14	MI	USA	USA
Fisher, Wayne	Boarder	M	12	MI	USA	USA
Jesse	Boarder	M	10	MI	USA	USA
Howlett, Agnes	Boarder	F	9	MI	MI	MI
Edwin	Boarder	M	7	MI	MI	MI
Laurence	Boarder	M	4	MI	MI	MI
Mack, Gertrude	Boarder	F	12	US	US	US
Beatrice	Boarder	F	8	USA	USA	USA
Mabel	Boarder	F	5	USA	USA	USA
Saunder, Norman	Boarder	M	8	USA	USA	USA
Richard	Boarder	M	6	USA	USA	USA
Spriggs, Alfred	Boarder	M	8	MI	USA	USA
Young, Raymond	Boarder	M	7	MI	USA	USA
Gonzeliss, Gabariel	Boarder	M	7	MEX	MEX	MEX

---

[82] Column headers used: Name, Sex, Year of Birth, Place of Birth, Father's POB and Mother's POB.

The James White Memorial Home for Aged Persons
Haskell Home Appeal, Vol. 1, No. 1 – Oct. 1897

Originally conceived to be part of the Orphanage, it was still tied to the Haskell Home in the S.D.A.s annual fund drive. The home was originally built by Elder James White who occupied rooms for some time. It was located at the corner of Aldrich and Lincoln Streets, north of the Sanitarium (See map on page 9). The house was repaired and enlarged to prepare it for the reception of the elderly residents. The building was three stories high and contained twenty-eight rooms. Bathrooms, a laundry, and rooms for an infirmary were added, and a steam boiler put in, so that it was both pleasant and comfortable. The location had ample grounds, pleasant surroundings and a lovely view. A broad veranda on the west and a small one on the south side gave residents the opportunity for access to the outdoor air for the feeble ones without the effort of walking far.

Typical Scenes in Homes for the Aged, Andrews University

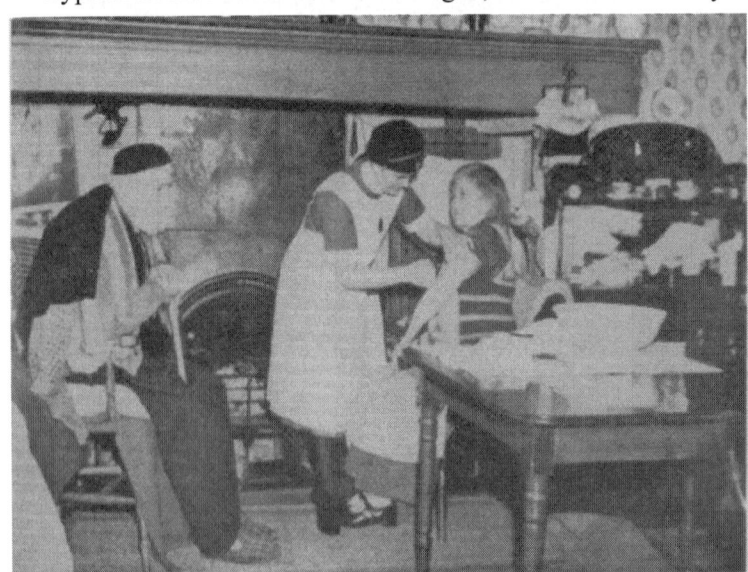

Rest for the Weary, Andrews University

The Haskell Home Cemetery
Or White-Thorn Cemetery

SITE OF THE
HASKELL HOME CEMETERY
Platted October, 1899 to serve the
Haskell Home, James White Memorial
Home, and other city residents.

Erected in 1989 by the families of
Villa Dell (Tefft) Collins
May 17, 1859 - Oct. 6, 1905
and
Dr. Lyman W. Henry
Feb. 26, 1817 - Oct. 29, 1904

Photos above from the collection of the author

For some time the need for a private burial ground for those who resided in the many benevolent establishments was needed and was platted in October 1899. It was restricted to inmates of the Haskell Home, the Old Folks' home and other destitute persons from the area. The remains from each institution were placed in separate sections apart from one another. Most markers were made of wood, or simply placing a small boulder to mark the final resting place of each loved one. The markers no longer exist but a memorial was dedicated on the site in 1989. The three victims of the 1909 Haskell Home fire are listed in bold print. ID is the FindaGrave.com Memorial ID that may be inserted on the home page to go directly to that persons memorial page.

Name	Born – Died	ID
John David Emanuel Artlip	Dec 1903 – Jul 8, 1905	142569961
Nina May Buell	May 1904 – Oct 15, 1905	142570598
Amy (Sheldon) Call	Feb 12, 1833 – Nov 22, 1909	70903971
Elvira M. (Warren) Childs	Mar 11, 1845 – Sep 4, 1910	70904011
Susanna (Zook) Clark	Aug 4, 1831 – Sep 3, 1902	70904039
Villa Dell (Tefft) Collins	May 17, 1859 – Oct 6, 1905	70904407
Cecil Coutant	unknown – Feb 5, 1909	70904121
Lemmul Ellis	Feb 24, 1830 – Mar 21, 1900	70905052
Grace Ellison	May 1823 – Feb 14, 1908	70904789
Joseph Guguere	Jan 6, 1816 – Mar 26, 1907	70904425
Gundar A. Gilbert	Jan 27, 1830 – Jan 26, 1903	70903931
A. B. Gomel	unknown – Jul 8, 1900	70904445
George Goodenow	1901 – Feb 5, 1909	70904139
Clara A. (Warren) Haas[83]	unknown – Jan 28, 1900	70904165
Lyman W. Henry	Feb 26, 1817 – Oct 29, 1904	70904206
Eva Grace Hopkins	Oct 7, 1899 – Sep 17, 1901	142566872
Eusebia Howlett	1805 – Dec 29, 1900	70904998
Sarah J. (Vooris) Hunt	Jan 19, 1824 – Sep 25, 1906	70904233
Clayton Huntley	unknown – Mar 23, 1902	142738352
Martha M. (Gale) Leech	May 29, 1832 – Jul 12, 1904	70904259
Louisa (Fowler) LeGay	Nov 28, 1810 – Feb 5, 1901	70904898
Eleanor McKelvey[84]	Mar 1, 1827 – Jun 20, 1917	70904808
Lena McKelvey	unknown – Feb 5, 1909	157002400
Calista (Clark) Moon	Jun 10, 1818 – Apr 9, 1909	142561023

---

[83] First known burial.
[84] Last known burial.

Name	Born – Died	ID
Anna Nash	unknown – Apr 4, 1900	70904433
Willard Kenneth Owen	Jun 6, 1911 – Jun 25, 1912	142563240
Margaret Phillis	Mar 14, 1842 – Feb 12, 1905	70904286
Alene Reedman[85]	1892 – Jun 19, 1895	142731329
Julia A. (Bicknell) Rhodes	Mar 5, 1832 – Apr 25, 1904	70904349
Sarah Ross	Jan 26, 1831 – Nov 7, 1901	70904911
Roy Sherman Rounds	Mar 30, 1891[86] – Aug 5, 1900	70903880
Lola Fern Sevy	Jun 8, 1903 – Sep 6, 1903	70903880
Carrie E. Smith	Sep 18, 1902 – Oct 7, 1903	70904378
Sarah (White) Thompson	Oct 14, 1825 – Dec 2, 1912	70904069
William Thompson	Nov 9, 1823 – Feb 16, 1905	70904090
Ethelyn Van Dervort	Jan 6, 1911 – Jan 30, 1911	142562533
Mary (Horton) Waterman	1815 – Jul 31, 1903	155376972
George W. Watson	Feb 17, 1907 – May 3, 1907	142571132
Donald Webber	Dec 26, 1908 – Aug 14, 1909	142561995

"HARRY OUR DARLING"
1940 photo of Haskell Home Cemetery
Courtesy of Willard Library

---

[85] Lena Redner is buried at Oak Hill cemetery, Lot 767, Rt 7.
[86] DOB computed from age, 9y, 4m, 6d in *The Haskell Appeal*, Vol 4, No. 1, Oct. 1900.

There were many obstacles in attempting to track down the orphans who left the Haskell Home at maturity and discovering what happened to the staff as they went their separate ways. There were inmates with common names that were found in adulthood, but no absolute link to connect them to the child at the Haskell Home. Females who married changed their surname. The same problem occurred when children were adopted and took their new family name as their own. This list if incomplete, but included in the hope that it may generate a more complete record of the orphans. Persons who survived the 1909 fire are listed in bold print along with their ages at the time of the fire. ID is the FindAGrave.com Memorial ID that may be inserted on the home page in the Memorial ID field.

Adelberg, Rosana May (1892-1969) AKA A'Delbert. At the Haskell Home in the 1900 census. Died 1969, buried in Hudson Corners Cemetery, Allegan, MI. ID 131744503.

Allen, Willie. Born about 1903, Michigan. At the Haskell Home in the 1910 census.

The Armstrong Family [Ancestry.com]
Front: William, **Pearl**, **Violet**, **Helen**, **Mary** (elevated), John R. (father)
Middle: **James**, Anna, Martha (Mother), Nell, **Herbert**
Top: Wesley, Dwight, Robert, Oliver [c. 1920s][87]

---

[87] Photos of Armstrong children from *Ancestry.com* except as noted.

Front: Dwight, William, John R. (father), Anna J., Wesley
Middle: Nell, Pearl, Helen, Violet, Mary
Top: James, Robert, Oliver, Herbert [c. 1930s]

Helen Izora Armstrong (10).   Born March 9, 1899 in Putnam, IA.   She married Andrew Graham Robb on June 25, 1917, in Marion, IA.   They had one child.   On December 12, 1924 Mr. and Mrs. Robb, along with their two-year-old son narrowly escaped serious injury when a 125-foot smoke stack on the plant of the American Products company next door crashed through their home in Detroit, MI.   All were cut and bruised by the falling bricks.   She died August 28, 1942, in Chicago.   All the Armstrong children were born in Iowa, from the union of John Robert Armstrong, born in Scotland, and Martha Hewitt Kerr, born in Ireland.

Herbert Samuel Armstrong, born March 18, 1896, Marion, IA.   At the Haskell Home in the 1910 census.   He married April 16, 1927, Goldie Goldberg, in Indiana.   Died April 28, 1966, Chicago, IL.   Photo: *Ancestry.com.*

SGT. HERBERT S. ARMSTRONG

James Lincoln Armstrong (14),[88] "the bicycle thief" later known as one of the heroes of the Haskell Home fire, served in World War I, assigned to Artillery in France.   Born January 16, 1895 in Marion, IA.   He married February 22, 1928, Eleanor Pearl Watson, in Garner, IA. They had three children. Died April 23, 1941, in a Fox Lake, Illinois car crash. Buried Grant cemetery, Ingleside, IL. ID 100614334.

PVT. JAMES L. ARMSTRONG
Cedar Rapids, Iowa
Born Marion, Iowa, January, 1894.
Wife, Ella. Son of Martha and J. R.
Armstrong. Artillery, France.

Mary Elizabeth Armstrong (15). Born in August, 1893 in Marion, IA. Her quick action was responsible for saving eight lives during the fire of 1909. She left the Haskell Home when she was seventeen and went to Chicago, IL. She married Hoyt A. Merritt on Sep. 18, 1913 which ended in divorce after living together for seven days. She was a nurse and labored unselfishly to the unfortunate. She worked valiantly during the great influenza epidemic of 1918 in Chicago, caring for hundreds of patients in their homes, for the hospitals could not care

for a tenth of the patients. She married Charles Augustus Wyrick, August 26, 1922, in Linn, IA. They had no children. Through the Depression years she remained a willing minister to the sick, the poor and the friendless. With her husband, they kept a rooming house at 303 South Loomis in Chicago's lower west side. When her husband died in 1951, she moved to Marshall, MI where two of her sisters lived. She died June 21, 1962, in Marshall MI, a patient at Oaklawn hospital since October 6, 1961. Buried in Forest Home cemetery, Forest Park, IL. Verified burial by cemetery office.

---

[88] Photo from Honor Roll, Cedar Rapids, Linn County, Iowa, p. 79.

Pearl Alice Armstrong (7).   Born October 24, 1901, in Linn, IA.   She married Raymond E. Bishop about 1924. They had three children.   Died June 8, 1992, Crawfordsville, IN.   She was the last known survivor of the 1909 fire.

Violet Martha Armstrong (10).   Born March 12, 1898, in Marion, IA.   She married Clair Arville Bordeau on April 6, 1918, in Battle Creek, MI. They had two children, celebrating their golden wedding anniversary in Marshall, MI in 1968. Clair Bordeau died in 1975.   She died August 31, 1990, Marengo, MI.   Buried Lyon Lake cemetery, Wrights Corners, MI. ID 102122225.

Sarah E. Bean.   Born 1858, Virginia.   Married Oct. 27, 1881, William Warr in Carthage, MO.   A former teacher, she was a Mother at the Haskell Home in the 1900 census.   She married Martin Dunn in 1922.   She died 1930 and buried in Sugar Creek cemetery, Mount Comfort, Hancock, IN.   ID 88217595.

Anna Marie Bjork.   Born April 19, 1892, Norway.   Immigrated to the United States in 1896.   She was a member of the Haskell Home in the 1900 census. Married June 24, 1911, Ironwood, MI to John Henry Green.   She was one of fifty-nine Sanitarium Nurses that graduated on May 12, 1920.   Death record not found. Photo: Ancestry.com.

Victor John Bjork.   Born c. 1890, New York.   He was a member of the Haskell Home in the 1900 census.   He was a clerk at the Battle Creek San.   Died Feb. 2, 1920, Battle Creek, MI.   Buried Oak Hill cemetery, Battle Creek, MI.   ID 15432035.

Lawrence D. Brown. Born 1895. He was a roomer at the Haskell Home in the 1900 census. His parents were missionaries to India where his father died, and his Mother returned to this country. Resided in Bloomington, IL and went missing Nov. 22, 1923, in Chicago, IL, after checking out of the Y.M.C.A. hotel, Sunday morning. His car was found in a garage near by. He was a man of excellent character and was in line for promotion at his employment. It was the opinion of the Chicago police that he had evidently "met with foul play  and his body thrown into the Chicago river, the graveyard of many missing persons." Died about Nov. 1924, Chicago, IL.   ID 196398765. Photo: *The Panagraph*, Bloomington, IL, Dec. 2, 1924, p. 15.

Winnifred Blanch Brown. Born July 9, 1892, Midnapore, India. She was a roomer at the Haskell Home in the 1900 census. Married June 26, 1912, Minor Hendryx. Died Dec. 13, 1935, Bloomington, IL. Buried Oak Grove cemetery, LeRoy, IL. ID 85564449.

Albert J. (Jack) Burrows, born April 25, 1874 in Pennfield township, MI, the fireman injured in the 1909 Haskell Home fire. Although there were no immediate articles following his injuries from broken glass lacerations in the 1909 Haskell Home fire, a "Remember?" column in the May 11, 1847 edition of the *Battle Creek Enquirer and News*, recalled that one of the city firemen, Jack Burrows suffered serious injuries. On the way to a 1904 fire at a boarding house, the left rear wheel of the combination wagon he was driving caught in the street car track and completely overturned the wagon, throwing Capt. Lloyd Evans about twenty-five feet.   Picking him up, the firemen, with the assistance of neighbors placed the engine back upon its wheels, and continued to the scene of the fire.   Albert became assistant fire Chief of the Battle Creek Fire Department in 1928. He died at his home on Highland Avenue, July 26, 1950. He was a member of the fire department for 38 years, retiring in 1942. The obituary mentioned his son, Don A. Burrows was the current battalion chief at the No. 1 station.   Buried in Hicks Cemetery, Pennfield, MI. ID 13449264.

Clarence James Chester. Born Feb. 12, 1889, Memphis, TN. He was a member at the Haskell Home in the 1900 census. Married Juanita, later divorced. Died Nov. 26, 1954, Blackman, MI. Buried Cherry Hill cemetery, Blackman twp., MI.

Steven Oleson Chovin (3). The little lad that travelled 200 miles from Worth, Michigan to the Battle Creek Haskell Home, in January of 1909, was born in March 25, 1905 in Michigan. In 1920 he was living in Bay, MI, with John and Arvilla Chovin. In 1930, he was living with the same parents in Allen Park, MI. He was a CBM in the U.S. Navy during WWII. He died July 21, 1966. Interred July 28, 1966 at Ft. Rosecrans National Cemetery, San Diego, CA. ID 3392229.

Oral Lee Clough. Born June 7, 1891, Sparta, MI. After the death of his brother Floyd (April 23, 1894), and the death of his Mother Mary (June 17, 1894), his father, Erastus, surrendered Oral and Lloyd, the twin brother of Floyd, to the American Educational Aid Association (Children's Home Society). Oral must have been transferred to Battle Creek before 1900 as he was a member of the Haskell Home in the 1900 census. Married June 18, 1914, Baraboo, WI to Lula Belle Barker. Died Oct. 30, 1966, Los Angeles, CA. Buried Green Hills Memorial Park, Rancho Palos Vereds, CA. ID 71297492.

Celestia D. Comins. Born 1849. She was a matron at the Haskell Home in the 1900 census. Died Oct. 1, 1916 at the Battle Creek Sanitarium, MI.

John Stephen Comins. Born 1844, Irving, MA. Married in 1878. He was the Super at the Haskell Home in the 1900 census. Died Oct. 3, 1916, Battle Creek Sanitarium, MI.

Ivan O'Dell Confer (10). Born May 21, 1898. Married August 26, 1928, Madalyn "Mattie" A. (Davis) Camburn on Battle Creek, MI. Divorced March 30, 1940, Calhoun county, MI. Married Jennie "Betty" Marina VanStrien on April 10, 1940, Calhoun county, MI. They had six children. Died Oct. 10, 1986, Battle Creek one of the last survivors of the fire. Buried in Reese Cemetery, Springfield, MI. ID 176631919.[89]

---

[89] Years later, Ivan Confer related that he and his late brother, Oren, were residents of the home when the blaze broke out. "We had been put in the home when our mother died. We had been there

Mabel Ruth Confer (8). Born 1901. She worked as a stenographer in Indianapolis, IN.

Oren Fredrick Confer (7). Born April 9, 1901 in Wayne, MI. Enlisted May 20, 1918 in the U.S. Navy, released May 15, 1922. Married March 15, 1924, Bernice F. Preston, Battle Creek, MI. They had five children. He was a Navy veteran of World War I. He was a charter member of the Bedford Rescue Squad, received his 30-year pin from Clark Tructractor, where he served as chief of plant protection, and conducted first-aid courses for many groups while earning his 30-year pin as a Red Cross volunteer. Oren was also clerk of the Battle Creek
Branch of the Church of Jesus Christ of the Latter-day Saints. He died May 30, 1981 in Springfield, MI. Photo: March 8, 1961 *Enquirer and News*.

Myrtle May Conner (8). Born May 10, 1899, Butler, MI. Married Mirle A. James, December 25, 1917, Calhoun co., MI. They had six children. Mirle died Oct. 16, 1864 in Coldwater, and she married Ehrl R. Crandall who died September 13, 1975. She died July 5, 1977, Coldwater, MI. Buried Fairview cemetery, Homer, MI. ID 68319473.

---

three years when the fire struck. I can still see James Armstrong waking up the boys. There were a dozen of us in the boys' dormitory. We got out by the stairs and in our nightgowns were herded with a bunch of girls through the snow to the old laundry building in the back. I can still see Miss Armstrong shoving some of the girls out the window of their wing onto the coal shed roof... I still can see the steamer fire engine, horse-drawn, lined up pumping. Well, the fire raged on. It burned out the structure and the big octagonal cupola fell through and we were homeless. But they set up beds in the old laundry and remodeled it and we lived on there some years. I was farmed out when I was 15 to an Elkhart, Indiana family where I remained until I was 21. Then I left Elkhart and came back here and found Oren had been in the Navy." *Enquirer and News*, Feb. 7, 1965.

Mabel Ruth Cooper (11) Born about 1897, Mt. Vernon, OH. Married Alfred Joseph Turgeon, May 7, 1919, Battle Creek, MI. They had at least one child. Husband was buried in Pine Grove cemetery, Lynn, MA.

Myrtie M. Dacon (11). Born August 23, 1897. At the Haskell Home in the 1910 census. Married Oscar O. LeClair, June 15, 1918, Battle Creek, MI. They had one child. Died October 12, 1965, Racine, WI. Buried Graceland cemetery, Racine, WI. ID 179875630.

Harry Earl DeWitt. Born March 12, 1905, Battle Creek, MI. At the Haskell Home in the 1910 census. Married July 8, 1926, Bessie B. Beebe, Grand Rapids, MI. Died 1992. Buried in Mount Rest Cemetery, Saint Johns, MI. ID 20807453.

Pearl DeWitt. Born about 1905, Michigan. At the Haskell Home in the 1910 census.

Berniece Ilene Edwards (6). Born June 16, 1903, Allegan, MI. At the Haskell Home in the 1910 census. Married Charles J. Choffin, October 6, 1923, Marshall, MI. They had at least three children. Died January 16, 1970, near Fort Madison, IA, coming home on a train from a visit to Tucson, AZ. Buried Hicks cemetery, Pennfield, MI.

Charles L. Hackney. Born about 1903, Michigan. At the Haskell Home in the 1910 census.

Jennie M. Hackney. Born about 1905, Michigan. At the Haskell Home in the 1910 and 1920 census. Married Charles Ross Mastin, April 22, 1922, Detroit, MI. They had at least one child. Divorced Jan. 14, 1927, Calhoun county, MI. Married Milo Nelson Crawford, 1930. Died June 20, 1986, Kalamazoo county, MI. Buried Mount Ever-Rest Memorial Park South, Kalamazoo, MI. ID 82708466.

Caroline Haskell died April 4, 1900 in Michigan City, IN and was buried in Ogdensburg Cemetery, Ogdensburg, NY, next to her husband. Dr. and Mrs. J. H. Kellogg attended the funeral which occurred in Michigan City on Monday afternoon, April 23, 1900. On a table in her upstairs room was a collection of pictures of interior views of the Battle Creek orphanage representing little tots in different situations of their motherless and fatherless lives. She stipulated in her will that the proceeds of her Chicago real estate holdings be distributed among a number of beneficiaries, including $10,000 to the Seventh Day Adventist Medical, Missionary and Benevolent Association of Battle Creek, Michigan, for the purpose of endowing the Haskell Orphanage Home of Battle Creek, Michigan.

Cady Haver. Born about 1888, New York. At the Haskell Home in the 1910 census.

Esther E. Herrick (9). Born about 1900, place unknown. At the Haskell Home in the 1910 census.

Francis E. Hill. She was born about 1900, Indiana. At the Haskell Home in the 1910 census. Living with Sarah A. Owen in Emmet, MI in the 1920 census as a county charge.

Harold K. Hill. Born about 1902, Indiana. At the Haskell Home in the 1910 census.

Edith Hostetler. Born Oct. 14, 1888, Manhattan, KS. At the Haskell Home in the 1900 census. She worked at the Battle Creek Sanitarium from 1901 to 1954. She attended the Seventh-day Adventists Church. Miss Hostetler died April 12, 1971 in Battle Creek, MI.

Edwin Bartle Hussey (4). Born October 10, 1905, Roswell, CO. Married Hilda M. McClain, May 3, 1924, Marshall, MI. He was

arrested January 11, 1928 on a charge of deserting his wife and three children, the second arrest for the same charge. Their eight-year-old son, Carl died August 30, 1933 at the University Hospital in Ann Arbor from an infected tooth. Edwin divorced Hilda M. on grounds of extreme cruelty, while she was serving a jail sentence in Marshall, MI for disorderly conduct in 1936. He received custody of their two children. He was inducted into the army at Fort Custer April 22, 1942 and promoted to corporal technician in August 1942. In April 1943, Sgt. Hussey was home on furlough. He served in France, discharged in December 1945. Member of the Veterans of Foreign Wars. Died

June 28, 1946, Battle Creek, MI, a week after he was struck while attending a meeting of the steel workers' union. The injury did not appear serious until his condition grew worse several days later. Buried Newbre cemetery, Battle Creek, MI, with military honors. ID 12844929. Photo: newspaper.

Dixon Ingels. Born about 1901, Nebraska. At the Haskell Home in the 1910 census.

Abbie Juckett. Born about April, 1909, Michigan. At the Haskell Home in the 1910 census.

George Lathrop. Listed as a survivor in the Feb. 5, 1909 *Battle Creek Daily Moon*. No further records found.

Calista B. McFarren. Born Jan. 1886 in Ohio. Her father was captured after escaping from an Ohio asylum. She was a member of the Haskell Home in the 1900 census, sister of Henry. She married Charles E. Banker Oct. 14, 1908. Battle Creek, MI. Divorced March 31, 1914 in Calhoun county, MI for extreme and repeated cruelty. She married Dec. 2, 1916, Gust. Alfred Johnson in Detroit, MI. Divorced Nov. 27, 1928 in Wayne county for cruelty. Enumerated with Gustav Johnson in 1930 and 1940 census in Detroit, MI.

James Henry McFarren. Born Jan. 22, 1892 in Bainbridge, OH. He was a member of the Haskell Home in the 1900 census, brother of Calista. In 1910 he was an apprentice harness maker boarding with Cora Willitts in Battle Creek.

Lulu Ruth Masten. Born Feb. 3, 1901, Bellevue, MI. At the Haskell Home in the 1910 census. Married Aug. 2, 1919, Claude Atwood DeLong, Detroit, MI. They had three children. Died July 13, 1980, Kalamazoo, MI. Not found on FindaGrave.com, but Claude DeLong is buried in Hicks Cemetery, Pennfield, MI, ID 13449728.

Charles Ross Moyer. Listed as a survivor in the Feb. 5, 1909 *Battle Creek Daily Moon*. No further records found.

Ruth Moyer. Listed as a survivor in the Feb. 5, 1909 *Battle Creek Daily Moon*. No further records found.

Frances Owen. Listed as a survivor in the Feb. 5, 1909 *Battle Creek Daily Moon*. No further records found.

Harold Owen. There were several articles regarding Harold Owen, born about 1892, that are included here, although there is no reference to his being the same Harold Owen from the orphanage. In a case of breaking and entering the house of Bert Moyer near Vicksburg, that went to the Michigan supreme court, Harold Owen was granted a new trial on appeal. Harold was convicted along with John Culp, his cousin, Milo Culp and Bert Dabbs of stealing peppermint oil valued between $400 and $500. These three were convicted and the Culps testified for the state incriminating Owen. Testimony proved that Owen was in his Battle Creek home at the time of the larceny, however, the oil was found in his possession a day later. The supreme court held that the trial judge was in error when he charged the jury with regard to an accessory before the fact while there was no evidence to show that Owen was such an accessory, as there was no testimony to show that Owen conspired with the other three in such a way as to make him an accessory before the fact. On January 7, 1928, Harold was convicted of participating in the theft and sentenced to Jackson Prison for a term of three to 15 years. John and Milo Culp had already completed their sentence given in October, 1926. He probably served the minimum sentence, as on August 2, 1931 he reported that his automobile had been stolen from West State Street.

Superintendent **Rodney Spencer Owen**. Born January 27, 1851, Ida, MI. He married Sarah Augusta Bordeau, August 4, 1875, Burke, VT. They had two children. He was in charge of the Haskell Home for six years. Died at his home on May 1, 1917, Emmett, MI, from pneumonia. Buried in Oak Hill cemetery, Battle Creek, MI. ID 19578767.

Matron **Sarah Augusta (Bourdeau) Owen**. Born May 18, 1856, Enosburgh, VT. Married Rodney S. Owen. Died Aug. 21, 1925, Cicero, IN. Buried Oak Hill cemetery, Battle Creek, MI. ID 19578768.

Bessie Partain. Born April, 1892 in Ladonia, TX. At the Haskell Home in the 1900 census. She was a member of the Seventh-day Adventist Tabernacle since 1909. Died Sep. 18, 1969. Buried Memorial Park cemetery, Battle Creek, MI. ID 84831209.

Ruth Ross (10). Born about 1899, Illinois. At the Haskell Home in the 1910 census.

Lillian Scott. Born about 1878, Wisconsin. At the Haskell Home in the 1910 census, as a helper, married about 1900 with three children;

Lloyd, Sylvia and Wilmer.

Lloyd Scott (7). Born May 11, 1901, Valmay, WI. At the Haskell Home in the 1910 census. Married December 13, 1924, Henrietta Lackershire, Menominee, MI. They had four children. Died March 28, 1944, Warren, MI.

Sylvia D. Scott (5). Born November 4, 1903, Sevastopol, WI. At the Haskell Home in the 1910 census. Married February 11, 1921, Robert Hollister, Detroit, MI. Married May 10, 1926, Fred Schiebner, Detroit, MI. Divorced Jan. 8, 1943, Wayne county, MI. Died June 8, 1965, Warren, MI. Buried Forest Lawn cemetery, Detroit, MI. ID 81680131. Photo: Ancestry.com.

Wilmer Francis Scott. Born April 18, 1909, Michigan. At the Haskell Home in the 1910 census. Served as Corporal, company B, 324th Engineers in World War II. Married Jan. 2, 1945. Claretta Elizabeth Diny, King County, WA. Died June 14, 1965. Buried Rock Island National Cemetery, Rock Island, IL. ID 2895801. Photo: Ancestry.com.

Haskell Home Orphanage (after 1909)
Photo from *Ancestry.com* (on Carl & Jesse Sprague page)

Carl Allen Sprague (7). Born April 7, 1902, Chelsea, MI. Married May 19, 1925, Betty H. Luce[90], Battle Creek, MI. They had no children. He began work with the Grand Trunk Railroad July 6, 1915, as a yard clerk and call boy, becoming a brakeman in 1920 and a conductor in 1936. Mr. Sprague was a member of the Order of Railway Conductors. Died April 29, 1956, Battle Creek, MI. Buried Oak Hill cemetery, Battle Creek, MI. ID 15326892.

Jesse Lewis Sprague (8). Born May 6, 1900, Weston, OH. In June of 1916, detective Peter Bhymer went to Fort Wayne, IN to bring back a man on the charge of stealing a wheel belonging to Jesse Sprague, the first time in years that a member of the police department travelled outside the state to make an arrest. The wheel had been stolen from Sprague during the previous week. Married August 6, 1923, Merceil Mary O'Grady, Battle Creek, MI. They had three children. Died June 21, 1974, Battle Creek, MI. Buried Mount Olivet cemetery, Battle Creek, MI. ID 9085277.

Kirk Randle Sprague (9). Born April 18, 1898, Providence, OH. Not married. Died May 25, 1943, State Hospital, Kalamazoo, MI. Body removed to Ann Arbor, MI Anatomical Lab.

---

[90] Married Elizabeth (Betty) Winn according to obituary of Carl A. Sprague.

Mrs. Almira S. (Dewing) Steele[91]. Born of puritan forebears in Chelsea, MA on July 23, 1842. She was reared in financial affluence and at an early age embraced the Abolitionist movement. In 1870 she married Walter Steele, businessman. His death three years later left Almira a widow with an infant daughter. She embarked on a personal ministry to care for and educate black children in the South. No orphanage existed for black children so in April, 1884 she founded the Steele Home for Needy Children, with three infants, in Chattanooga, TN. This institution quickly fell into controversy and was destroyed by arsonists. Undaunted, she erected on the site a substantial three-story, brick Queen Anne building that had forty-four rooms.

As a Congregationist turned Seventh-day Adventist, she served her wards a vegetarian diet and held church services Saturday and Sunday. The children received a "Christian education combined

[91] https://tennesseeencyclopedia.net/entries/almira-s-steele.
https://en.wikipedia.org/wiki/The_Steele_Home.
For more photos see cityscopemag.com/city-scope/ask-hamilton-15.

with industrial training." Adolescent students were sent to various trade schools or colleges. She managed the Steele Home for forty-one years, and between 1884 and 1925 she sheltered and educated more than sixteen hundred children. Mrs. Steele, because of her benevolent work was known the world over. Railroads, recognizing her good work provided her with free transportation. She sought treatment at the Sanitarium for a broken wrist, her first vacation in twenty-eight years, and became a great friend of Dr. and Mrs. John H. Kellogg. She brought with her several children from the home and placed them in the Haskell Home. Over the years she sent 128 of her finished students to the Haskell Home, the Sanitarium, the Battle Creek College. She died at the Sanitarium following a heart attack, June 6, 1925.

Cecil Stephony. Born about 1899, Wisconsin. At the Haskell Home in the 1910 census.

Melvin Stephony. Born about 1904, Wisconsin. At the Haskell Home in the 1910 census.

Walter Taylor. Born Jan. 1894, Illinois. At the Haskell Home in the 1900 census. He was a stone cutter in a monument factory in Coldwater, MI for twenty years. Died Oct. 5, 1947, in a tuberculosis sanatorium in Clyde, OH, where he went about a year before his death.

Howard Francis Waller. Born September 14, 1898, Battle Creek, MI. Not married. Died July 3, 1917, after a lingering illness. Buried Mount Olivet cemetery, Battle Creek, MI. ID 11021621.

Chester Arthur Watson. Born March 1, 1899, Ashtabula, OH. At the Haskell Home in the 1910 census. Married Nov. 4, 1918, Constance M. King, Battle Creek, MI. Died July 30, 1928, Battle Creek, MI. Buried Spaulding Cemetery, Eaton County, MI. ID 97845783. Photo: FindaGrave.com.

Manuscript Collections

Center for Adventist Research. Andrews University, Berrien Springs, MI.

Davis, Glenn and Jean. *The Haskell Home Cemetery.* 1989. Helen Warner Branch of Willard Library.

Helen Warner Branch, Local History. Willard Library, Battle Creek, MI.

Historical Society of Battle Creek Archives. Battle Creek, MI.

Welch, Shirley Annette. *The Haskell Home.* Andrews University. Fall, 1975.

Magazines

Atteberry, Maxine, "Seventh-day Adventist Nurses: A Century of Service." *Adventist Heritage* 8, no. 2 (1983): 3-11.

Butler, Mary G. "The Village of Battle Creek: 'Distinguished for Its Love of Liberty and Progress.'" Heritage Battle Creek 9 (Winter 1999):23-30.

Hook, Milton Raymond. *Flames over Battle Creek.* Washington, D.C.: Review and Herald, 1977.

Jenkins, Gary C. "Almira S. Steele and the Steele Home for Needy Children," *Tennessee Historical Quarterly* 49 (1989): 29-36.

Schwarz, Richard W. "The Kellogg Schism: The Hidden Issues." *Spectrum* 4 (Autumn 1972): 23-39.

Books

Butler, Mary, et al. *The Battle Creek Idea: Dr. John Harvey Kellogg and the Battle Creek Sanitarium* Heritage Publications, 1994.

Chapman Bros. *Portrait Biographical Album of Calhoun County, Michigan.* Chicago, 1891.

Gardner, Washington, ed. *History of Calhoun County.* Chicago: Lewis, 1913.

History of Calhoun County, Michigan. Philadelphia: L. H. Everts, 1877.

Kellogg, John Harvey. *The Battle Creek Sanitarium System: History, Organization, Methods*. Battle Creek, MI: n.p., 1908.

Lowe, Bernice B. *Tales of Battle Creek*. Battle Creek, MI: Miller Foundation, 1976.

Oursler, Fulton and Will. Father Flanagan of Boys Town. Doubleday & Co., Inc., Garden City, NY, 1949.

Principles of the Battle Creek Sanitarium. Battle Creek, MI: n.p., n.d.

Salomon, Otto A. *The Theory of Educational Sloyd*. 3rd ed. Boston; Silver Burdett, 1906.

Schwarz, Richard W. "John Harvey Kellogg: American Health Reformer." PhD diss., University of Michigan, 1964.

Van Buren, A. D. P. "The City of Battle Creek: Its Early History, Growth, and Present Condition." *Michigan Pioneer and Historical Collections* 3 (1881): 347-67.

——————. "Pioneer Annals: Containing the History of the Early Settlement of Battle Creek and Township." *Michigan Pioneer and Historical Collections* 5 (1884): 237-93.

Newspapers

Battle Creek Daily Journal
Battle Creek Daily Moon
Battle Creek Enquirer and Evening News
Battle Creek Enquirer
Battle Creek Evening News
Battle Creek Journal
Battle Creek Moon
Battle Creek Moon Journal
Battle Creek Nightly Moon
Battle Creek Tribune Citizen
Daily Chronicle
Daily Journal
Daily Moon

Detroit Free Press
Detroit News
Enquirer and News
Evening Chronicle
Evening News
Expounder
The Haskell Home Appeal
Kalamazoo Gazette
Marshall Daily Chronicle
Marshall Statesman
Medical Missionary, The
Michigan Tribune
Nightly Moon
Review and Herald

Made in the USA
Columbia, SC
05 December 2024

48455510R00091